THE DEFENSE OF GRACCHUS BABEUF

Joachim Bateuf 9/50 1964 Cornea

THE DEFENSE OF GRACCHUS BABEUF

BEFORE THE

HIGH COURT OF VENDOME

EDITED & TRANSLATED
BY
JOHN ANTHONY SCOTT

———————

WITH AN ESSAY
BY
HERBERT MARCUSE

———————

& ILLUSTRATIONS
BY
THOMAS CORNELL

SCHOCKEN BOOKS · NEW YORK

First published in a limited edition
by the Gehenna Press in 1964

First SCHOCKEN PAPERBACK edition 1972

Copyright © 1967 by The University of Massachusetts Press
Library of Congress Catalog Card No. 67–11244
Manufactured in the United States of America

TO SIDNEY KAPLAN

CONTENTS

LIST OF ILLUSTRATIONS

BY JOHN ANTHONY SCOTT

François-Noël Babeuf was born on November 23, 1760 in the parish of St. Niçaise, near the town of St. Quentin in the province of Picardy.[1] Babeuf's father Claude, of whom we know very little for certain, led a humble and impoverished life at one time as a village tax collector and at another as a common laborer. François-Noël knew hardship and poverty from his earliest childhood, and it is even doubtful that he ever went to school. At about the age of fifteen, he went out into the world to earn his own living and help contribute to his family's support.

During the following years Babeuf worked as apprentice and servingman with various employers. In November 1782 he married Marie-Anne-Victoire Langlet, an unlettered maidservant of the seigneur of Daméry; in the following year he made his home in the town of Roye, where he began to follow the profession of keeper of manorial rolls. Seven children were born to Babeuf and his wife, but parenthood amid the turmoil of revolution was for them a tragic experience. Three girls and a boy died at tender ages. Two more boys, Camille and Caius, perished in young manhood. Only one child, Emile, survived to a ripe age.[2]

In the years preceding the Revolution, keeper of the manorial rolls was an important job. Throughout France the land was burdened with an incredible variety of taxes and dues. The aristocracy, increasingly impoverished and chronically in need of money, looked upon its traditional rights with a jealous eye, seeking in every possible way to maintain and extend them. Keepers of the manorial rolls, or *commissaires à terrier*, were paid to ransack the archives and furnish legal evidence to buttress the insatiable demands of a parasitic nobility upon the tillers of the soil. The job was comparatively well paid and from 1785 until the outbreak of the Revolution Babeuf lived in comfortable circumstances. "Such was the situation," he later remarked, "in which I laid bare, amid the dusty archives, the repulsive secrets of the nobility and the story of its usurpation of the land of France."[3]

For Babeuf affluence and security were short-lived. In 1789 the Revolution swept into the discard *commissaires à terrier* along with the nobility and the survivals of feudalism. The rest of his life, some eight years, would be devoted to an unrelenting political struggle, waged amid the direst poverty, often in hiding, and punctuated for months at a time by periods in jail.

On learning that the Bastille had fallen, Babeuf hastened to Paris, remaining there until the October days, when the people marched out to Versailles

demanding bread. He made the trip primarily to see to the printing and publication of a book calling for the abolition of all the antiquated feudal forms
of taxation and the substitution for these of a single-tax system—the famous
Cadastre perpétuel.[4] By October 5 his mission had been accomplished and he
went back home. For the next three years, until February 1793, Picardy
remained the main center of his revolutionary activity. These years were
characterized by a tenacious and unremitting struggle for the abolition of
all forms of oppressive taxation by Church or by State, by nobility or by
municipality, in that province. During this time Babeuf was condemned to a
jail term (served in Paris) for advocating abolition of the government excise
and salt taxes; launched his first newspaper, *Le Correspondant Picard;* cir-
culated pamphlets and petitions advocating the abolition of feudalism and
the division of public lands; and defended persons brought to court for refusal
to pay taxes or feudal dues. He won wide popularity at the same time as he
incurred the enmity of the aristocracy, and in September 1792 was elected
to the administrative council for the department of the Somme. Revolutionary
ardor, at a time when the movement for the abolition of the Crown and the
institution of the Republic was in full swing, led him to substitute the name
of a small farmer for that of an aristocrat in a legal document transferring
ownership of a confiscated estate.[5] Babeuf's enemies seized upon this blunder,
drove him from his office, and hauled him before the courts. In February 1793
he fled to Paris to escape prosecution; and thus it came about, almost by acci-
dent, that Babeuf from that time on played out his revolutionary role on the
national rather than on the provincial stage.

For over six months, from April to November 1793, Babeuf held a post in
the Paris municipal administration's *bureau des subsistances,* which was responsible for the provisioning of the capital. But his enemies were powerful,
and on November 14, 1793 he was arrested upon complaint made to the Paris
authorities by the public prosecutor of Montdidier. From that date until the
summer of 1794 Babeuf spent most of his time in jail, either in Paris or Laon.
In the meantime his penniless family lived upon the verge of starvation. On
July 18, 1794 Babeuf was released at the direction of the Laon court and he
returned to Paris.

Babeuf's liberation coincided with the arrest and execution of Robespierre,
the destruction of Jacobin control of the Republic, and the institution of the
thermidorian reaction. The overthrow of Robespierre, which occurred on

FRANCOIS MARIE AROUET DE VOLTAIRE

July 29, 1794, spelled the unfolding of an effort, on the part of conservative members of the *Convention nationale,* led by Tallien, Fréron, and Barras, to bring the Revolution to an end. But this was not clear to Babeuf; he shared, in the first days after thermidor, the widespread illusion of the Paris workers and *sansculottes* that the fall of Robespierre would inaugurate a movement to give back to the people the democratic rights promised them by the Constitution of 1793, but that had never materialized owing to the emergency of war and wartime dictatorship. *Sansculotte* hostility to Robespierre during the final months of his rule may be traced to Jacobin persecution and liquidation of popular leaders like Hébert and Chaumette, to a permissive attitude toward war profiteering, and to the setting of a ceiling upon wages. When, therefore, Babeuf launched his *Journal de la liberté de la presse*[6] in September 1794, voicing sharp criticism of Robespierre and of the excesses of the Terror, he agitated in favor of basic democratic rights, with especial emphasis upon a free press and a return to the Jacobin Constitution of 1793.

Babeuf's illusions about the beneficent motives of the men of thermidor were rapidly dissipated. With the twenty-third issue, on October 5, 1794, the *Journal* changed its title to *Tribun du Peuple, ou le défenseur des droits de l'homme,* parted company with its thermidorian printer, Guffroy, and launched open warfare upon thermidor.[7] Babeuf was at once arrested; though he was released soon after, his supporters in the political *club de l'Evêché* were scattered and he himself, driven into hiding, was obliged to publish his paper in secret. His attacks on the men of thermidor became increasingly sharp;[8] on January 29, 1795 Tallien demanded his arrest from the floor of the Convention. Tracked down by the police and seized early the following month, Babeuf was first confined in Paris and then transferred to Arras on March 15, where he remained a prisoner until September 10. At Arras the government had concentrated, in the *des Baudets* and *Providence* prisons, a number of ex-Jacobins and *sansculottes,* among them Charles Germain, a young man of twenty-five years who was to be one of the future leaders of the *conspiration.* These men communicated with each other freely over the long months; they discussed the problems which the Revolution faced and the political perspectives which they should adopt. The prisons of Arras were the revolutionary school in which the *conspiration pour l'égalité* was first conceived and given shape.

The *conspiration* was to occupy the remainder of Babeuf's days. In 1797

4

he would pay with his life for the major part that he had played in its conception and organization. What, then, were the goals he sought? What philosophy underlay his revolutionary action?

Babeuf's political theorizing may be traced back to 1785, when he submitted to the Royal Academy of Arras a memorandum that resulted in a long correspondence with its secretary, Dubois de Fosseux. This exchange reveals a man already familiar with the speculative and critical philosophy of the eighteenth century and passionately concerned to apply the ideas of that philosophy to the solution of the social problems of his own day. Babeuf's thinking proceeded from a very concrete basis. Himself a servant of the declining feudal system and its beneficiaries, he had witnessed at first hand the reality of gross social inequality, of an irrational economic system, and of grinding poverty. As one whose function it was to discover the law and help his masters apply it, he saw in the legal structure an instrument to perpetuate the domination of the landowning class and to protect a cruel and inequitable system of private ownership. As early as 1786 he had asked himself the question whether, utilizing the sum total of human knowledge, it would be possible to sweep away the existing order and to establish a society where full economic, social, and political equality would prevail. At least two years before the outbreak of the Revolution he had reached the conclusion that such an objective was fully practicable.[9]

The next step would be to decide *how* to reach this goal, and then to elaborate the *form* of organization, in both society and State, requisite for the maintenance of an egalitarian social order. The Revolution itself provided Babeuf with the experience from which his answers to these questions would be fashioned.

The first years of the Revolution saw the unfolding of a tremendous struggle in the countryside for the abolition of feudal dues, services, and taxation. Babeuf strove to widen and deepen this movement, and to give it direction. He appeared in the first instance as a leader of the peasantry in the struggle against these exactions, but this was for him only a beginning.[10] The struggle against feudalism and for a just tax system might arouse the masses and precipitate them into social struggle, but it would not by itself solve the fundamental problem of French society. No revolution, in Babeuf's view, could be considered complete that did not result in the abolition of private property and of the division of society into exploited and exploiting classes. In 1791 he had formulated this demand as a central revolutionary objective to be raised and publicized when the time was ripe. Land division—in the terminology of the French Revolution, the *loi agraire*[11]—would, he thought, be for French people an important first step toward a society without class differences and without exploitation.

Between the movement for immediate reform—land, equal taxation, universal compulsory education, minimum wage laws, and the like—and the realization of vaster revolutionary transformations, there was in Babeuf's eyes a political link of the highest importance. This link was the institution of a democratic republic, a democratic constitution, and an appropriate system of supporting law. Babeuf had a great deal to say about many of the aspects of democratic philosophy and legal theory; much of this found a focus in his insistent and sustained demand for freedom of the press, and it is the only aspect of the matter that can be touched upon here. Already in the first days of the Revolution, in his *Correspondance de Londres*, Babeuf had fulminated against the efforts of the Paris municipality and of the police to curb free expression of thought in speech and writing. In his own first journalistic venture of the years 1790–1, *Le Correspondant Picard*, he had learned from first-hand experience the power of the press and its indispensability in a popular campaign. Robespierre and the Terror drew his fire in 1794 for the curbs that the Jacobins had placed upon a free press and free speech. In Babeuf's view the fullest political rights and the broadest political democracy were to be conquered and defended not principally as ends in themselves, good though they might be. Freedom of thought, of press, of debate, and of political action were in his view of value primarily because only when they enjoyed these rights to the full could the people find their way to a better social order; could overcome the obstacles involved in engineering its creation.

It was precisely on this question, political freedom, that the Revolution reached a crisis while Babeuf at Arras sat in the *prison des Baudets*. In May 1795 came news of the great uprising of prairial, when the people of Paris, goaded by starvation, took matters into their own hands, rose against the government, and suffered defeat and bloody retaliation. Babeuf was electrified by this news; far from being discouraged, he took it as evidence of a new upsurge of the populace and a renewed opportunity for revolutionary struggle.[12] In September news came that the men of thermidor had secured ratification of a new constitution, the Constitution of the year III. So far from putting into effect the stillborn Constitution of 1793, this was a huge step backward, spelling the indefinite postponement of universal suffrage and setting up a system in which France would be legally ruled by a wealthy and powerful *élite*.[13] On September 4, 1795 Babeuf issued a manifesto in which, denouncing the new Directory and the tyranny of the rich, he called for the overthrow of its new Constitution.[14]

A few days later, on September 10, Babeuf was transferred to Paris and incarcerated in the *prison du Plessis* in company with many other revolutionaries, ex-Jacobins, and *sansculottes*—among them Filippo Buonarroti—who would later be found in the *conjuration*. On October 18, 1795 Babeuf was amnestied and released. His great hour had come: to rally the people of Paris in a struggle first for the democratic Constitution of 1793 and then for the resumption of the Revolution's forward path.

On November 5, 1795 Babeuf resumed publication of the *Tribun du Peuple*. At the same time he and his *sansculotte* friends came together with dissident members of the *Convention nationale* like J.-B. Drouet and ex-Jacobins like Félix Le Peletier.[15] They set up the *club du Panthéon* for the pupose of carrying on open agitation for the overthrow of the Directory and for a return to the old democratic order. The *Panthéon* held crowded meetings in the *salle des Génofévains* and probably attracted thousands of adherents. Its success was its nemesis. A frightened government ordered its dissolution; on February 27, 1796 Napoleon Bonaparte drove out the membership and barred the doors. The *Tribun du Peuple* was once more proscribed and declared illegal. The Pantheonists were not arrested, but they were driven underground. In the spring of 1796 the government increased the severity of its repressive measures against the opposition. Henceforth the only remedy was to work in secret, and thus the *conspiration pour l'égalité* was born.[16] In March 1796 an underground directorate was set up which included Babeuf, Filippo Buonarroti, Sylvain Maréchal, Félix Le Peletier, and A.-A. Darthé. It began to prepare plans to rally the people of Paris and to bring about the overthrow of the established government. Gracchus Babeuf, leader of the peasantry, had become an organizer of the *sansculottes*.

The *sansculottes* were defined by contemporaries as "men who possess, as it were, no means of livelihood other than the work of their hands."[17] The workers of Paris in the last decade of the eighteenth century constituted a labor force of somewhat under 65,000, working for the most part in small

7

shops or for petty employers—there was an average of 16 to 17 workers per employer. The most important occupations were not, as today, in heavy industry. The vast majority of the workers were employed in the construction trades (painters, plasterers, roofers, glaziers, masons), in light industry (textiles and other fabrics), and in services.[18]

Since the outbreak of the Revolution the *sansculottes* had, at intervals, played an extremely important political role. Often spurred on by hunger the people of Paris had come out on to the streets again and again in support of broad revolutionary demands and in protest against famine and the high price of bread. The Revolution received, for example, great impetus from the mass movement of July to October 1789, which culminated in the march to Versailles and the hunger protest of the October days. Again, the fall of the monarchy in 1792 was directly due to the intervention of the Paris masses; and the rise of the Jacobins in 1793 was based upon *sansculotte* support, just as surely as their collapse was due to the alienation of the Parisians in 1794. April and May, 1795—the days of germinal and prairial—brought a resurgence of the workers' movement in the form of a massive protest against famine and thermidorian reaction. But after the bloody repression of these hunger demonstrations the *sansculottes* lapsed into a dull passivity. It was Babeuf's task to awaken them, to inspire them, and to lead them back to the barricades.

The thermidorians maintained themselves in power by the use of a network of spies, by police arrests and repression, by laws illegalizing political opposition, and, in the last resort, by the use of force to crush popular uprisings.[19] Babeuf and his colleagues understood that such a government could only be gotten rid of by the use of popular force. Accordingly they set about arming themselves and the people, and they set the day for a new *levée en masse*. Agents were dispatched to every part of Paris to carry on propaganda, to organize discussions, and to raise the morale of workers and soldiers alike. The *Tribun du Peuple,* appearing at irregular intervals, discussed both immediate objectives and ultimate revolutionary aims.[20] The *sansculottes* were reached daily by an effective system of *affichage*—the placarding of posters and handbills, and the dissemination of leaflets and pamphlets. People of Paris, people of France, hear this! For centuries you have lived in slavery; like the rest of mankind you have been pawns of tyranny and greed. Now you have risen up and you have made a revolution to achieve the age-old

8

JEAN-JACQUES ROUSSEAU

dream of equality, brotherhood, and peace. Now it is time for the rich and the powerful, for those who sit on thrones and those who give the law, to listen. The people want more than the mere dream of equality, of freedom. The present revolution is only the curtain-raiser to another, yet more fundamental social change. We, the people, want equality and the Constitution of 1793, the democratic Constitution which we truly deliberated upon and truly accepted as the legitimate source of governmental authority.[21]

The *conjurés* also opened communications with the provinces, and encouraged agitation wherever they had connections—in the Pas de Calais, Arras, St. Omer, Béthune, Lyon, Reims, Châlons, Sainte-Menehould. Guided in part by the experience of the Terror and of war dictatorship, they worked out the form that the State should assume immediately after the Directory had been driven from power—a revolutionary dictatorship based upon peasantry and *sansculottes* under arms. The new government would institute pressing reforms including the division of lands, the progressive tax, equal and universal public education.

The government became frightened by the speed with which the movement grew and the scope that it assumed. One of its ubiquitous agents, a Captain Grisel, who was stationed at the Grenelle military camp, was admitted to a meeting of the secret directorate on April 30. A wave of arrests followed early in May. Babeuf and Buonarroti were picked up in Babeuf's headquarters on the *Grande-Truanderie* amidst a plethora of documents which would provide the government with its proof.

On August 27 the *conjurés* were sent in iron cages to stand trial before a specially constituted High Court. Vendôme, in the Loire valley, was designated as the place where the Court should sit in conformity with a constitutional provision that forbade it to hold sessions in Paris. The trial opened in the Vendôme *Palais de Justice* on February 20, 1797.[22] The accused numbered sixty-five, but eighteen of these were tried *in absentia,* including Félix Le Peletier and J.-B. Drouet. Of the forty-seven defendants present, the majority were *sansculottes,* who gave their professions as laceworker, embroiderer, clockmaker, printer, turner, goldsmith, weaver, shoemaker, etc. The Court was composed of a president and four associate judges, and the case was tried before a sixteen-man jury chosen by electoral assemblies in the departments.

Babeuf and his colleagues were tried under a law of April 17, 1796, which had been framed specifically to cope with the rising tide of revolt against the

10

Directory. This law decreed the death penalty for advocacy by word or in writing of the overthrow of established authority, of the re-establishment of the Constitution of 1793, or of the division of lands. The mandatory death penalty caused a problem for the defense. Babeuf was in favor of openly admitting the fact of conspiracy and of utilizing the forum of the Court to defend and justify it before the French people; but his co-defendants pointed out that under such a defense the jury would have no alternative but to find them all guilty and the Court to condemn them all to death. The tactical problem, therefore, was how to defend the *conjuration* as a political movement against a tyrannical government while saving as many as possible of the defendants' lives.

Babeuf's solution to this problem was, on the one hand, to deny the *actuality* of conspiracy but, on the other, to defend the *right* of revolution against a tyrannical government. Refused the right to counsel of his own choice—he would have chosen the revolutionary journalist, P. N. Hésine—Babeuf conducted his own defense. In April 1797 he delivered a courtroom address which lasted for three consecutive sessions—about three days—and constituted the supreme literary and forensic effort of his career. In this document, written out in full in his own hand, he summarized a lifetime of revolutionary thought and action.[23]

On May 24, 1797 Babeuf and A.-A. Darthé were found guilty of advocating the re-establishment of the Constitution of 1793; on May 26 they were sentenced to die.[24] Seven others, including Buonarroti, were found guilty on the same charge and sentenced to deportation. With family shattered and dreams broken, Babeuf wrote a last farewell to his wife and children. "I feel," he said, "no regrets that I have given my life for the best of causes. Even if all my efforts shall have been in vain, I have done my duty."[25]

Babeuf and Darthé were executed on May 27, 1797.

*   *   *

Babeuf divided his defense into four parts. In the first, after giving a detailed explanation of the causes that had thrown the *sansculottes* into opposition to the Directory, and of the reasons that had led the Babouvists to take action against it, he discussed the right to revolution and the circumstances that led the conspirators to feel that the time had come to exercise it. In the second and third parts, after discussing the mass of documents which the Government had seized at the time of his arrest and which it offered as proof of the

11

existence of a conspiracy, he submitted his own explanation of the meaning of this material. In the final part Babeuf, delivering his own personal defense, in contrast to the "general defense" that had preceded it, insisted upon the thesis that "independently of the proof of the non-existence of a conspiracy ... I was not a conspirator."[26]

Selected for translation in this volume is the first part of Babeuf's "general defense,"[27] for it contains the heart of his plea and constitutes in its own right a document of great value for the historian of the French Revolution, for the political scientist, and for the student of Babeuf's life. To it has been added Babeuf's famous trial peroration, *si cependant notre mort est resolu; si l'horloge a sonné pour moi....*[28]

Babeuf's *Defense* has value because it helps us to place its author not only in the context of the Revolution to which he made so huge a contribution, but in the context of the entire modern age. Babeuf was one of those giant figures whose life and thought sum up one epoch that is past and illuminate another which is to come. The *Defense* shows us that he was deeply indebted to the outstanding thinkers of the Enlightenment for his social concepts, and principally to Rousseau, Helvetius, Mably, and Morelly; and that, both through these thinkers and beyond them, he had assimilated the contributions of the greatest theorists and reformers of the western world from Plato to Sir Thomas More. But Babeuf did not merely utilize the thought and the example of these people: he stood upon their shoulders. He took the utopian critique of private property as the root of pride, violence, poverty, and war; fashioned the dream of a society where wealth is held in common and all grow rich together;[29] and convinced himself and others that struggle to realize this ideal was a practical, realistic objective for men and women to give their lives to.

The *Defense*, for the rest, illuminates the motivations of Babeuf and his fellow-conspirators, brings to life an extraordinary personality, and constitutes the last utterance of a tragic being who refused to accept human misery and human injustice, and was ready to die for his beliefs.

In the course of the *Defense* Babeuf quoted from various writings, including his own. In some cases, as in the citations from Morelly, his memory served him well and the quotations were word for word accurate. Other quotations cannot be traced with such exactness; Babeuf was often obliged to paraphrase the thoughts of his authorities, and this, of course, is not difficult to understand. The defendants were obliged to prepare their case under great handicaps; the government afforded them few facilities, and Babeuf, who did not even have a lawyer to represent him, was in no position to look up sources or to check references.

The names of all persons mentioned by Babeuf in the course of the *Defense* have been included in the Biographical Notes, which also list the names of the principals in the *conjuration* together with those of other individuals mentioned in this introduction. A translation of the *conjuration's* fundamental propaganda document composed by Sylvain Maréchal in 1796 and widely distributed among the people of Paris, the *Manifeste des Égaux*, follows Babeuf's defense.

[1]The literature on Babeuf's life, ideas, political relationships, and revolutionary action is extensive. His own published writings are listed in Victor Advielle, *Histoire de Gracchus Babeuf et du babouvisme d'après de nombreux documents inédits* (Paris, 1884), I, 475–518; and in Maurice Dommanget, *Pages choisies de Babeuf* (Paris, 1935), 3–10. Dommanget also indicates (10–11) the most important archival sources. Original documents have from time to time been reproduced in the French historical journals; note especially V. M. Dalin, "Un inédit de Babeuf: sa correspondance de Londres," *Annales historiques de la Révolution française*, XXX (April-June, 1958), 31–59, and Gabriel Deville, "Notes inédites de Babeuf sur lui-meme," *La Révolution française*, XLIX (1905), 37–44. Much of Babeuf's correspondence has been printed, but there is no available listing. Advielle reproduces over a dozen letters in full (vol. I); a modern edition of Babeuf's literary exchanges with Dubois de Fosseux is available—*Correspondance de Babeuf avec l'Académie d'Arras* (1785–88), edited by Marcel Reinhard (Paris, 1961), but this does not include the crucial draft of June, 1786 discovered in the Moscow archives in 1960. For a number of very important letters, see also Dommanget; Georges Bourgin, "Quelques inédits de Babeuf," *Annales historiques,* XXXI (1959), 146–53, 252–69; and Louis Jacob, "Corres-

pondance avec Babeuf," *ibid.* XI (1934), 253–9. Correspondence with Guffroy is reproduced in *Révolution française*, VIII (1885), 733–6 and LXXXII (1929), 6–24. For a letter to Danton of July, 1790 see *Annales historiques*, II (1925), 488, and XXX (Oct.–Dec., 1958), 84–5.

For the secondary literature the excellent critical bibliography of Dommanget, 11–33, must be supplemented by Jacques Godechot, "Les travaux recents sur Babeuf," *Annales historiques,* XXXII (1960), 369–87; and Claude Mazauric, "Bilan des études sur l'histoire du mouvement et de l'idéologie babouviste," *Rivista storica del socialismo,* V (June–Aug., 1962), 63–82.

[2]Through much of Babeuf's work runs the persistent theme of the agonies of fatherhood in a world cruelly indifferent to the needs of children. See, for instance, his remark about his daughter Sophie, who died in 1795: "one day there came to me in prison the shattering news that she had died of starvation following the reduction of the bread ration." *Défense générale devant la Haute-Cour de Vendôme*, Advielle, II, 69.

[3]G. Babeuf, *Tribun du Peuple, à ses concitoyens* (Paris, an III), 1.

[4]*Permanent land registry, or an explanation of the procedure necessary to carry*

13

through this important work, in order to guarantee equitable assessment and distribution of the tax burden, and the simple collection of a single tax both upon landed property and personal income (Paris, 1789).

⁵This was the affair known as the *faux*, or forgery. See Abel Patoux, "Le faux de Gracchus Babeuf," *Société académique des sciences, arts...de St. Quentin, série 4*, XVI (1913), 140–209. For this offense, which Patoux terms "a revolutionary crime," Babeuf was condemned, August 23, 1793, to twenty years in chains.

⁶*Journal of Freedom of the Press*, nos. 1 to 26, Sept. 3 to Oct. 12, 1794, were printed by A.-B.-J. Guffroy, a deputy to the Convention. No. 23 in the series bears the new title *The Tribune of the People, or Defender of the Rights of Man*.

⁷In a letter to Babeuf of October 12, 1794 Guffroy bitterly denounced Babeuf's change of political line, and accused him of preaching radical propaganda. "Henceforth," he wrote, "we can no longer make common cause. Henceforth I will not be your printer." *Révolution française*, LXXXII (1929), 5–10.

⁸In nos. 28 and 29 Babeuf warns of the danger of rising reaction, and states that there are two Republics—the Republic of the rich and the Republic of the poor. He calls for a return to the Constitution of 1793, an end to the war, the distribution of land.

⁹Babeuf, writes one authority, has by 1787 "constructed from the dreams of egalitarian philosophy a plan for the future; he has reached the conclusion that only the triumph of a society where absolute political and social equality prevail, can put an end to the misery that he sees around him, and to the sufferings which have been part of his own life experience." Albert Thomas, "La pensée socialiste de Babeuf avant la conspiration des Egaux," *La Revue socialiste*, XI (1904), 236. See also *Correspondance de Babeuf avec l'Académie d'Arras* (1785–88), and V. M. Dalin, "Babeuf's Social Ideas on the Eve of the Revolution," *Novaia i noveisha istoriia* (1961), translated in *Soviet Studies in History* (Winter 1962/63), 57–72. The view of the matter set forth by Thomas and elaborated by Dalin contradicts the position taken by C. Mazauric [*Babeuf et la conspiration pour l'égalité* (Paris, 1962), 66], who concludes that the evidence shows Babeuf to have been in these years "egalitarian rather than collectivist."

¹⁰"I confined myself," he wrote of his work in Picardy, "to fighting the most crying and deeply resented abuses. The hydra of feudalism, scourge of our countryside, provoked a general uprising....I came out as the champion of all the country people against the lords of the land." Babeuf to Sylvain Maréchal, Paris, March 28, 1793. Advielle, I, 106.

¹¹The Roman *lex licinia agraria* of 377 B.C. set a maximum upon the amount of land that any one person could own, and decreed the division of surplus lands to those who had too little or none.

¹²"You and I and all patriots," he wrote to Fouché from Arras on April 8, 1795, "must not conceal from ourselves the fact that the results may turn out badly for us. But should we allow ourselves to be discouraged? No! Genius and courage blossom in the hour of danger." Advielle, I, 130.

¹³The Constitution, wrote Charles Germain to Babeuf from Arras on July 2, 1795, was of use only to "the greedy caste of rich owners who batten on the people and grow fat upon their misery." *Ibid.*, I, 137.

¹⁴*Deuxième lettre à l'armée infernale et aux patriotes d'Arras*. Advielle, I, 167–70.

¹⁵For the story of J.-B. Drouet's relationship with this movement, see Louise Lévi, "Le retour de Drouet," *Révolution française*, LXIX (1916), 400–26. The best available account of Le Peletier is Philippe Dally, *ibid.*, LXIII (1912), 193–213.

[16] For the history and organization of the *conspiration* see Filippo Buonarroti, *Conspiration pour l'égalité dite de Babeuf*, Robert Brécy and Albert Soboul, eds., 2 vols. (Paris, 1957). This includes a number of original documents, more of which are reproduced in *Copies des pièces saisies dans le local que Babeuf occupoit lors de son arrestation*, 2 vols. (Paris, 1797), and in Corps Legislatif, *Extraits du procès-verbal*, 12 prairial, 23, 25, and 29 floréal, an IV (Paris, 1796). The most valuable studies of the *conspiration* are Maurice Dommanget, *Babeuf et la conspiration des Egaux* (Paris, 1922); Gabriel Deville, *Thermidor et Directoire* (Paris, 1904); A. Galante Garrone, *Buonarroti e Babeuf* (Turin, 1948); and Samuel Bernstein, *Buonarroti* (Paris, 1949). The periodical literature is extensive; part is listed in Dommanget, *Pages choisies*, 36–42. Very little on the *conjuration* has appeared in English beyond Bronterre O'Brien's translation of Buonarroti (London, 1836); Belfort Bax, *The Last Episode of the French Revolution* (London, 1911); and Samuel Bernstein, "Babeuf and Babouvism," *Science and Society*, II (1937–8), 29–57, 166–94.

[17] Petition of the *société populaire de Mende*, Lozère, January 28, 1794, in *Annales historiques*, XXVI (1954), 363.

[18] See the interesting figures assembled by F. Braesch, "Essai de statistique de la population ouvrière de Paris vers 1791," *Révolution française*, LXIII (1912), 289–321. For a helpful brief survey of the role of the Paris worker in the Revolution, see also George Rude, "Les ouvriers parisiens dans la Révolution française," *La Pensée* (May–Aug., 1953), 108–28.

[19] See Richard Cobb, "Note sur la repression contre le personnel sansculotte de 1795 à 1801," *Annales historiques*, XXVI (1954), 23–49.

[20] Babeuf resumed publication of the *Tribun* on November 5, 1795, or little more than two weeks after his release from *du Plessis*. Nine numbers appeared between then and the close of the series, April 13, 1796.

[21] This is a brief paraphrase of the two fundamental propaganda documents of the *conspiration*: the *Manifeste des Egaux*, and the *Analyse de la doctrine de Babeuf*. For translation; see above.

[22] Official trial publications are listed in Jean Dautry's bibliography, *Conspiration pour l'égalité, op. cit.*, II, 224–6. Babeuf's *General Defense* was not published in the official record of the trial, but the manuscript survived and was reproduced in full by Advielle, II, 1–322. The concluding portion of Buonarroti's defense was published for the first time in *Annales historiques*, XXXIII (1961), 56–73.

[23] Dommanget thought that the defense tactic "trapped Babeuf and prevented him from showing his full measure." *Pages choisies*, 303–4. The virtual omission of the *General Defense* from this work is a serious weakness in it.

[24] "I can no longer feel anything for my family!" wrote Babeuf to his dearest friend on hearing the verdict; "I suppose that this comes from the awful feeling that all the struggles I have undertaken for them are in vain. Bloody reaction will take vengeance on our kith and kin! And then, again, this joyless existence withers the passionate heart. There is a limit beyond which human endurance cannot go." Babeuf to Félix Le Peletier, Vendôme, May 24, 1797. *Bibliothèque historique de la Ville de Paris*, reproduced in *Annales historiques*, XXVIII (1956), 307–9. This version supersedes those of Advielle and Dommanget.

[25] Last letter to his wife and children. Advielle, I, 339.

[26] Part 4 of the defense is published in the court record, *Débats du procès instruit par la Haute-Cour de Justice contre Drouet, Babeuf, et autres* (Paris, 1797), 362–78.

[27] Advielle, II, 11–65.

[28] *Ibid.*, II, 320-2.

[29] Babeuf's concept of the socialist state and its organization has for long been the subject of an unresolved controversy. See especially Alfred Espinas, "Babeuf et le babouvisme," *Revue internationale de sociologie*, VI (1898), 305-50; Albert Thomas, "La pensée socialiste de Babeuf"; Georges Lefebvre, *Etudes sur la Révolution française* (Paris, 1954), 298-304, 305-314; V. M. Dalin, "Babeuf's Social Ideas"; R. N. C. Coe, "La théorie morellienne et la pratique babouviste," *Annales historiques*, XXX (1958) 38-50, together with the "colloque epistolaire" that follows 50-64; A. Saitta, "Discussion sur le communisme en 1796," *Annales historiques* (1960), 426-35; Jean Dautry, "Le pessimisme économique de Babeuf et l'histoire des utopies," *Annales historiques* (1961), 215-33; and Mazauric, *Babeuf*, 145-77.

THE DEFENSE OF GRACCHUS BABEUF

Gentlemen of the Jury,

Never, perhaps, at any time or among any people in recorded history has a trial been held more momentous than this. Never before have such world-shaking issues been presented for decision to a court of justice. And never did a court exist, aside from the court of public opinion itself, more fit and proper than this to pronounce an authoritative verdict.

Your findings are sought in a case that is intimately linked with the fate, with the very survival of the Republic and of all who cherish it. The freedom of the French people—whether it will retain its sovereign independence or whether it will be forced to live upon its knees in a base and degrading slavery— is here at stake.

Gentlemen of the jury! You are members of the finest of our institutions to escape the onslaught of reaction. You represent the people. You are high and independent magistrates, who have been assigned the task of defending human rights and human freedom from the plots and conspiracies that may be set on foot against them. You are, in the first instance, guardians of our rights against the encroachments of the State and of its appointed officials. Rise, I urge you, to the challenge of your majestic function. In so doing, you will reflect honor upon yourselves. You will vindicate the right of honest men to follow freely the dictates of their conscience. You will be the saviors of your people.

But this case involves more, even, than the fate and future of France. Natural right and positive law are also involved. Their meaning, as decided here, will either ensure the triumph of reason and sanity among men or postpone it for a millenium or more. Whoever has followed this trial attentively will have no difficulty in seeing that the advocacy of dangerous ideas, rather than a conspiracy against constituted authority, is under indict-

19

ment here. These ideas the ruling class deems inconceivably dangerous; dangerous, because such ideas are subversive of the power and the privilege that our rulers have themselves usurped; dangerous, because they are based upon self-evident truths and elementary notions of justice, and may, therefore, all too easily spark a revolutionary fire among the masses. Of this our leaders stand in mortal dread.

My voice, long silenced, is to be heard at last, in these last moments before the time of judgment comes. That judgment will decide my fate, the fate of my comrades who have suffered with me, and the fate of many, many more who are doomed to follow in our footsteps if this great drama ends in the tragedy which some seem so passionately to wish. Without further ado, therefore, I shall set before you the nature of the burning grievances that I have voiced, and that bring me to this bar.

I have dared to entertain, and to advocate, the following doctrines:

The natural right and destiny of man are life, liberty, and the pursuit of happiness.

Society is created in order to guarantee the enjoyment of this natural right.

In the event that this right is not so guaranteed to all, the social compact is at an end.

To prevent the dissolution of the compact, a fundamental right is reserved to the individual.

This is none other than the right of every citizen to be vigilant against violations of the compact, to alert others when they occur, to be the first to resist tyranny, and to urge others to follow the same course.

From this follows the inviolable right of the individual to think and to communicate his thought to others; to keep a jealous

CLAUDE ADRIEN HELVETIUS

watch that the social compact is followed to the letter in conformity with the natural rights of man; to rise up against usurpation, oppression, and tyranny; and to show men ways of putting an end to such excesses on the part of their rulers and of winning back the rights that have been lost.

This is the doctrine for which alone I have been put on trial. Anything else charged against me is only a pretext.

We who stand at this bar are certainly not the first men whom the rulers of the earth have persecuted for reasons much the same. Socrates made war on bigotry—and drank the poisoned cup. Jesus of Galilee, who taught men to love equality, truth, and justice, and to hate the rich, was nailed alive to the stake. Lycurgus fled his native land to escape death at the hands of those whom his deeds had made happy. Agis, the only just man ever to be a king, was put to death because he made an exception to the law. The Gracchi were slaughtered at Rome, and Manlius was hurled from the Capitol. Cato opened his veins. Barneveldt and Sydney mounted the scaffold. Margarot has been wasting his life in the desert, and Kosciusko rotting in the dungeons of St. Petersburg. James Weldon had his heart torn out. Michel Le Peletier, in our own Revolution, perished under the assassin's knife. I mention no other name than his, since, to quote his brother—yet another brother of the glorious martyr—who composed the fine plea on behalf of Félix Le Peletier, our co-defendant: "Michel Le Peletier, alone among the martyrs to liberty, may be recalled without rekindling the fires of factional strife."

Some of these heroes whose names I have just mentioned were put to death in accordance with the forms of law. But their position before their judges, gentlemen of the jury, was rather different from our position here. None of the courts before which these men were tried had the majesty of yours. It is true that many of our rights have been violated here, and that we have been deprived of many safeguards to which we are entitled. And yet it has not proved possible to deny us the protection of the finest of republican institutions which, as I have already noted, has suffered least of all from the onslaught of the counter-revolution. You, gentlemen of the jury, still remain to serve and defend the people. Our sublime system of law permits adequate scope for the defense of persons accused of crime. Notwithstanding all sorts of obstacles and difficulties, our defense is endowed with a breadth and significance that would have been unthinkable in the case of any of the great men whose names I have mentioned. Nearly all of them were condemned by so many courts-martial! Two hundred and eighty-four members of the Areopagus passed sentence upon Socrates, to be sure; but they were the creatures of two vile scoundrels, Anytus and Meletus, and Socrates did not defend himself. Christ's trial amounted to nothing more than a brief interrogation by Pontius Pilate. The Ephors wasted little time before handing Agis over to his executioners. Sydney, Margarot, and Weldon heard sentence pronounced only a few moments after they appeared before their judges.

One must admit that in the present case the prosecution has been obliged to proceed more circumspectly. For this the credit must go, in the first place, to our laws, which prescribe a careful and time-consuming procedure in all trials involving a capital offense; and, in the second place, gentlemen of the jury, credit is due to your own wishes, to your desire to seek out and to find the truth no matter what the cost. For yours is a serious responsibility. There is no higher court set over you to review your verdict. You are answerable at the bar of history alone, in the presence of all who love truth, justice, the inalienable Rights of Man, and the sacred cause of human freedom.

Personal considerations do not prompt me to thank you for the conscientious way in which you have undertaken to sift the issues in this complex affair. Nor are personal considerations involved when I appeal to you to listen with close attention to what I have to say. Many years have passed since I made the decision to dedicate my life—yes, and if necessary to sacrifice it—to the revolutionary struggle. There is little reason for me to prolong an existence made bitter by oppression, by the rigors of prison, and by the hatred of so large a number of wicked men. On the contrary, there is a consolation in dying for the sake of truth, justice, honor. To die a martyr does not cut short a man's life; such a death, rather, confers immortality, for the man who dies in such a cause lives on in the hearts of his people. Love of country, gentlemen of the jury, nothing else, makes me beg you to put forth the greatest efforts to master the facts of this case. Only this will enable you to reach a just verdict.

It cannot be said too often that this trial is the trial of the Revolution itself. The fate of the Republic hangs upon the issue. Royalism lies in wait at the doors of this sanctuary. Hawklike, it watches what happens here. It reports the proceedings in the minutest detail, gives them its own special slant, and distributes its propaganda among thousands of devotees who pant for the moment when sentence shall be pronounced. Tremble at the thought of it, you who love mankind! For then the hour of vengeance will strike. Throughout the length and breadth of France death and outlawry will be decreed for republicans. The events of floréal[1] have already served as an excuse for their persecution. My name has already acquired the odious distinction of designating a sect which includes all republicans, all patriots, and

24

which is charged with preparing them all for the establishment of a new reign of terror. Gone are the epithets of Robespierrist, Terrorist, Anarchist, and Jacobin: *Babouvist* has taken their place.

For the moment, to be sure, our enemies are in doubt about the issue of this trial; they have curbed their savagery a little and stayed their hands. But the truce that they have granted will last only until the scaffold has been set up. When that time comes, the witch-hunt will start again. The name of the arch-conspirator Babeuf will be used as a bugbear to spread far and wide the confusion and the demoralization that have already jeopardized the Republic's survival. The friends and partisans of freedom will become victims of despairing panic and political paralysis. Royalist steel, paraded with a licence more brazen than any it has yet enjoyed, will rid the earth of the republican race. Swiftly and surely royalism will set a term to the revolutionary interregnum when France was free of the Capetian yoke.

The first to be marked for immolation will be the several thousand good citizens whose names are listed in my so-called notebooks as presented in evidence by the prosecution. This is a sad prediction, but it may all too easily come true, like so many others that have been made during the Revolution by wise but reluctant prophets.

Nor is that all. I must say again, the effect of a calamitous issue to this trial will be felt far beyond the confines of the Republic. Natural law, the inalienable Rights of Man, and the sovereign rights of a free people are issues central to the case here under consideration. How can such issues ever again be discussed anywhere, if the highest tribunal of a nation reputedly free brands the discussion as subversive and punishes the participants as monsters and heretics? Who will be rash enough ever again to risk his life in teaching those great truths, without whose light mankind is doomed to wander in the dark night of ignorance, bowed down by ever-growing and—as it seems to them in the darkness where they are—unavoidable sufferings?

I am well aware that in this last observation I reveal the secret of the people's weakness and the corresponding strength of their would-be oppressors. My words, indeed, might provide them with a commentary upon a theme by Machiavelli. But the knowledge of human weakness does not increase the strength of the oppressor; and I do mankind no harm in calling attention to this weakness here. I do this in order to underline the conclusion—which I think, gentlemen of the jury, that you have been able to reach by yourselves—that this case is one of inexpressible importance; and that you will do well to give me your closest attention in the argument that it is my desire and my duty to lay before you.

In a democracy, yes, even in Rome, I would be brought before the people themselves, in the public square, to argue my case. The people themselves would decide whether I or any of my co-defendants were guilty of treason. The people themselves would decide whether there was any evidence that a conspiracy had actually been set on foot against them, as alleged in the horrifying—or, to say the least, extremely serious—accusation that has been levelled against us. The people themselves would decide whether there was any evidence of any intent to subject the nation to the dictatorship of a single tyrant or of an oligarchy —either of which would be equally criminal. And the people would decide whether there was a design to sacrifice the masses to the desires of the few, to base an empire of idle, parasitic wealth upon the bondage, misery, and shame of honest and innocent toilers. As far as I can see, this is the only kind of con-

DENIS DIDEROT

spiracy that can be directed against the people. More than that, a conspiracy not directed against the people cannot be a conspiracy at all.

These considerations, furthermore, are the only ones which the people would have to take into account in determining the guilt or innocence of the defendants at this trial. If our intentions, as manifested in our daily activities, our speeches, and public proceedings, indicated nothing but a sustained and dedicated struggle for an objective the exact opposite of the criminal purposes that I have outlined above; if, that is to say, we manifested a devoted, constant, and passionate concern for the people's welfare, and for the curbing, by means of a wise social system, of the evil passions which might henceforth work corruption in the nation and tarnish its glory; if we were brought before the people and could succeed in convincing them that we were innocent of any crime but the desire to promote their happiness, then I make no doubt but that the people would absolve us of guilt, declare us to be loyal patriots, and silence the wicked and traitorous men who have dared to libel and oppress us.

But in a country the size of France the people themselves are not able to constitute the court and sit in judgment upon those who are accused of conspiracy and subversion. Judicial authority must of necessity be delegated: and hence the institution of a national jury system.

The term, People's Court[2] is entirely appropriate for such a jury, quite apart from the rest of the state apparatus that surrounds it. With this qualification I grant the accuracy of the definition which its skillful author has given us. In you, gentlemen of the jury, I see the true judicial representatives of the French people, empowered to pass upon a case of national importance and to judge as the people themselves would judge, in conformity with the people's own true interests. Such is the popular institution that I see here before me. I see in you a group of delegates from all parts of the Republic who in my eyes represent the people; who, symbolically, are the people, and before whom I must speak and act as I would before the people themselves. I would like to believe, gentlemen of the jury, that you hear me as the people would hear me, with the people's heart and soul.

It is necessary for me to organize my defense in accordance with a definite plan. Since I am charged with having a hand in every part of the alleged conspiracy, I am obliged to deal with it in its general aspect. Hence it will suit me to follow the prosecution's sequence in its indictment of 6 ventôse.[3] I shall compare the successive charges with the evidence that emerges from an analysis of the documents and from the information developed during the course of the trial itself; I shall try to show you that the indictment is baseless, although, to be sure, cleverly conceived. I shall demonstrate the emptiness of this mountain of vague conjecture and the shakiness of a scaffolding erected almost exclusively upon guesswork, probabilities, and presumptions. I shall demolish lock, stock, and barrel the whole pack of imaginary crimes and nightmarish plots.

My name first appears in this affair linked with that of Drouet. This circumstance does me no dishonor. To be associated with the man who founded the Republic, who restored to national control the regime that succeeded fourteen centuries of royal tyranny, and who took energetic steps to consolidate that regime —such a thing, I say, can furnish the defendants here with nothing but an honorable recommendation in the eyes of true friends of liberty.

It is to be noted that other names, equally dear to the people, are found in the list of the accused. We find here, for example, the brother of the illustrious Le Peletier who sacrificed his life for love of the people and hatred of their oppressors. Our association with the Le Peletiers will discredit us only in the eyes of kings and their creatures. Yet such are the men that the prosecution has picked upon as the alleged leaders of a conspiracy *against* the Republic! Who, in his senses, could even believe such a thing? These are the men who founded the Republic, who devoted their lives to it. To defend it, they have faced death; and for its sake they have suffered death. Is it possible that such of them as survive could have devised this monstrous plan to wreck their own handiwork, brought into being at so great a cost in blood, and agony, and struggle? Such a thought is the wildest of follies, and it is simply not to be taken seriously.

But a fresh surprise is in store. The indictment goes on to state that there are only two questions before this Court for its decision. The first: Is it an established fact that a conspiracy was actually organized with the intent to overthrow the government? The second: Are the accused, as named, guilty of participating in or organizing that conspiracy?

Was the prosecution anxious to remove from the Court's consideration the question of the moral justification of the facts before it? The question of a man's motive, or intention, is an entirely proper one for judicial determination. Examination of motive, indeed, is a basic right of the accused. Rule out this right and you thrust us back into the barbaric procedure of the *ancien regime*. You take us back to the days when the despot need only decree that such and such an act was to be considered a crime, and an offender was found guilty automatically, no matter what the circumstances.

30

The central question to be decided here, in my opinion, is whether the actions which the prosecution has called a conspiracy against the Republic did, in effect, constitute one. The Court must decide whether certain plans which were thought out, but which could not be translated into reality owing to the lack both of practical means and of mass support, were anything more than idle, humanitarian dreams—the last thing in the world to be branded with the stigma of criminal intent.

As for myself, I have from the beginning been singled out as the arch-conspirator. To be sure, the prosecution felt obliged to say (at the opening of the indictment of 6 ventôse) that "it will only be possible after the trial to ascertain precisely the role that each of the accused played;" but it did not hesitate to assert, even before the trial had actually begun, and in this very same statement, that "it is established and proven, beyond a peradventure, that a CONSPIRACY TOOK PLACE." These last three words are printed in capitals on page two of the indictment. The government, evidently, wished to establish in the jury's mind a presumption of guilt even before the trial began. It wished to prevent the jury from entertaining the slightest doubt, with or without the offer of proof, that a serious crime had actually been committed.

What was the object of the conspiracy? It is stated again on page two of the indictment: "to destroy the government, to overthrow the established authorities, to massacre a huge number of ordinary people, and to organize the looting of private property." What a sensation this charge must have made at the time it was originally published! Time and reflection have placed matters in a saner perspective and people now know better what to believe. I may recall to your minds the feelings of fear and anger that this first government statement was designed to provoke; I do not need to make an effort to allay such feelings.

Let us then turn our attention to the facts in this case, noting the difference between the prosecution's version of these facts and our own.

At the outset the prosecution undertakes to define "the crime of conspiracy and the precise characteristics by which it may be recognized." I shall find it necessary to examine very carefully what the prosecution has to say on this score.

The prosecution begins with some strange thoughts, which it calls "considerations on the Revolution." This they were obliged to do in order to lay the groundwork for their subsequent conclusions. In order to vilify the men who made it, the Revolution had to be presented as a catalogue of crimes suffered too long to go unpunished. The Revolution's greatest days, when it triumphed over all its enemies, when it vindicated gloriously the rights of the people, are here portrayed as harbingers of dire calamity. The end of the bigoted rule of priests is bewailed because it has led to the spread of "atheism." Those happy changes confidently expected as a result of the establishment of the Republic are dubbed "anarchy." Those measures that were dictated as a means of breaking the resistance of the country's enemies are branded as chaos, murder, and robbery. Laws for the relief of misery are seen as nothing more than red ruin. Those who rallied to the defense of the Republic are pilloried as murderers, anarchists, evildoers, monsters newly emerged from their hidden lairs. "All these self-styled patriots," the statement continues brazenly, "are the very same who have torn, mutilated, and devoured their native land."

Starting as we do from opposite premises, it is hardly to be wondered at that the defendants should differ radically from the

HONORE DE MIRABEAU

prosecution and should reach opposite conclusions. What they call the worst of evils is in our eyes the greatest of goods; what they call a vile crime is to us the height of virtue. They shed tears over the sorrow that the Revolution has brought to a handful of the overprivileged. We, on our side, groan at the sufferings which the masses have undergone throughout. We weep over the starvelings whom death has taken, over the no less hapless ones that death has spared, and over the innocents whom the dirty frauds of bankruptcy, financial trickery, and demagogic intrigue have stripped of their last rags. The prosecution makes moan over a handful of victims from the ranks of the favored few. We are moved to compassion by the thousands of republican citizens who have poured out their blood to defend France against the invader, and by the thousands more whom cruel reaction has slaughtered with impunity. The accumulation of power and privilege in the hands of a tiny minority already rendered formidable by reason of its wealth alone, and the slavish subjection of practically the entire people to this handful of the mighty—this the prosecution calls *order*. But we call this *disorder*. *Order* is only thinkable to us when the entire people are free and happy.

To desire the overthrow of *order* in their meaning of the word and to substitute *order* as we have defined it, this, according to the government, is to *conspire;* conspiracy, say they, is to will the overthrow of *established government*. This definition, in these exact words, is given on the first two lines of page six of the indictment. But is this really a correct definition? And, in the present case, does not everything turn upon a correct definition of this word, *conspiracy?*

Elsewhere in the indictment, to be sure, it is implied that actual conspiracy must be distinguished from the intent to overthrow "legitimate authority." And at various times during the course of the trial Citizen Bailly has informed us that conspirators are those who desire the overthrow of a Constitution "freely adopted by the people," under the pretext of establishing a better regime. There are various differences of meaning in these divers statements. But it is quite certain that to overthrow established government, legitimate authority, and a Constitution freely adopted by the people, are not one and the same thing.

The greatest error in all politics is doubtless the idea that the essence of conspiracy consists in the intent to overthrow established governments. If this were true, the peoples would be doomed to remain for all time under any government, no matter how base and vile, that had once succeeded in establishing itself. Such reasoning flouts the principle of the sovereignty of peoples; it is nothing more than a new version of the divine right of kings. From this viewpoint the Revolution of July 14, 1789, which overthrew an established government, was a criminal conspiracy.

Less erroneous is the assertion that conspiracy is the intent to overthrow legitimate authority or a Constitution freely adopted by the people. But let there be no misunderstanding on this score: these two things are still by no means the same.

To work for the overthrow of a Constitution freely adopted by the people could still be far from conspiracy. The people might, with apparent freedom, have adopted a radically vicious Constitution. Lack of proper information might have prevented them from recognizing this. In such an eventuality it would be no crime to show the people how to improve matters; such a thing would be no more than the performance of a work of public education and enlightenment. The first and basic prerequisite of human association is the recognition of an implicit right to improve the social and political system in order to promote the happiness of its members. This right is usually unwritten, but it is absolutely inalienable. The people are never to bind themselves against their own true interests; they are never to place shackles upon themselves; nor are they to devise laws to shackle future generations. In agreeing to abandon the state of nature and on becoming a member of society, each man has in effect relinquished his primordial independence solely in order to improve his lot. Society, in other words, is committed to an unending quest for human welfare, and every man, woman, and child is to reap his or her fair share of the social reward that is the fruit of social cooperation.

To enter into a conspiracy in order to bring about the overthrow of legitimate authority—this, we might say, would indeed constitute a truly subversive act. What, exactly, is legitimate authority? In my view it is authority established in accordance with the true principles of popular sovereignty; which governs in accordance with those principles; and which dedicates itself to the welfare of the nation, to the enhancement of its glory, to the defense of its freedom. He who dares to conspire against such authority and to enthrone despotism in its stead is guilty of a great crime. But he who, no matter how good the established government may seem, asserts that a still better one is possible, such a man is guilty of no crime at all, even though he is in truth mistaken. He is, in fact, engaged in nothing more than advocacy.

Now that these truths have been established, it is time to ask: Are we, the accused in general, guilty? Am I in particular guilty of having conspired against legitimate authority and of having sought the overthrow of a Constitution freely adopted by the nation?

The nature of this case, gentlemen of the jury, has occasioned

JEAN-BAPTISTE DROUET

the conduct during the trial of a kind of course in public law. Issues of the greatest delicacy, which in times such as these could not possibly have been openly debated anywhere else, have been solemnly canvassed here in this Court. While I cannot undertake to examine all that has been said upon these great issues, I cannot avoid attempting at least some analysis of them.

In truth, I have not conspired secretly against established authority, but I cannot deny that I have spoken out against it loud and long. In view of the fact that "the written word is to be understood as the instrument used to carry through a plan of insurrection which was the main object of the conspiracy" (indictment, page 23), and in view of the fact that the government is prosecuting for conspiracy even those who are alleged merely to have distributed such writings, if only as accessories to their production, I suppose I must be deemed a participant in the conspiracy. I am obliged, therefore, to justify my thinking and to set forth the considerations which have governed my actions.

As I have noted above, to will the overthrow of legitimate authority and to will the overthrow of a Constitution adopted by the people are not the same thing. I return to this distinction.

Legitimate authority presupposes a Constitution as perfect as can be expected from human devising. It postulates the recognition of all the established principles of human law, of all those rights that protect the practice and the enjoyment of freedom and of popular sovereignty. But, as I have postulated above, the people might freely adopt a Constitution which still did not give complete sanction to human rights. We could not, in that case, designate as legitimate a government deriving its authority from this fundamental law. Legitimate authority is derived solely from that Constitution which gives recognition to the principles of national freedom and sovereignty. Legitimate authority can be derived in no other way.

From this it follows that I have no more than a single question to deal with in order to establish two conclusions. When I admit, that is, that I sought to enlighten the people concerning the true worth of the existing regime, I strove to prove two propositions: first, that the existing Constitution does not guarantee the inalienable rights of the people; and second, as a necessary consequence of this, that the government deriving its authority from this Constitution does not possess the degree of legitimacy appropriate to the government of a free people.

I saw, in the existing government, the sovereignty of the people slighted, and the right to elect and to be elected granted exclusively to a small minority. I saw the revival, not merely of ancient privilege, but of new and odious distinctions between active and passive citizens. I saw all the guarantees of personal freedom swept away—the right of petition and of assembly, the right of the people to bear arms, the right to a free press. What was worse, I saw the people's sacred, inalienable right to make the laws taken away from them and vested in a Second Chamber; and this notwithstanding the fact that throughout the entire Revolution the bicameral system had been so long and so bitterly opposed. At the same time I saw the Executive vested with great power and removed from popular control—it was even given the power to remove the popular representatives and to replace them at its discretion. I saw social services and public education completely ignored.

How different was the state of affairs before! The previous Constitution had been overthrown and the present one had been established against the wishes of the people. The previous Constitution had been sanctioned by 4,800,000 votes, cast freely, decisively, and almost unanimously. The existing one was propped up by at most 900,000 votes, cast under the most dubious circumstances.

Such are the grounds for my contention that, if indeed I did conspire, it could not have been against legitimate authority, nor contrary to the general will of the French people.

I think that I have already shown what it means to conspire against legitimate authority, and I have already set forth the thesis that my political purposes, so far from being directed against such authority, had, on the contrary, been devoted to the effort to bring such authority into being and to aid in its establishment. In order to give you a fuller understanding of this fact it will be necessary for me to go into considerable detail; and I shall proceed, therefore, to explain to you the nature of the political and revolutionary mission which I felt called upon to fulfill.

The prosecution has traced the origins of the alleged conspiracy to my newspaper *Tribune of the People,* which has been in circulation since 13 vendémiaire.[4] The prosecution, indeed, has built a major part of its case around the publication of this journal. Not a few of the defendants who sit before you have been dragged here on no other grounds but that they have been supporters, readers, subscribers, distributors, or what have you, of the *Tribune.* Evidence, too, for the existence of the selfsame alleged conspiracy has been found in the doctrines that I have given voice to in this paper; in the theories of the general welfare that I have expounded in its columns; in the concepts of true social equality which I have set forth in its pages; and in the picture of public woe which—the prosecution asserts—I took it upon myself to paint in exaggerated colors, and the blame for which I laid falsely at the government's door—falsely, forsooth, because the evils described were really only "the result of circumstances." Last but not least, the prosecution has charged that "these writings were used as tools of the revolutionary action which was the central object of the conspiracy." I must speak, then, of all these things as necessary details, or even an essential part, of the charge against me. I must speak of all that has influenced me, all that has led me to proclaim the facts and ideas that are held against me.

After 13 vendémiaire I became aware that the masses—weary of a Revolution whose twists and turns had brought them only sorrow—had, it must be admitted, turned back to royalism. In Paris I saw that the simple and unlettered people had been led by their enemies to feel a cordial detestation for the Republic. The masses, whose judgment is guided by daily experience, had with little difficulty been induced to ask themselves: How did we fare under the Crown, and how is it now under the Republic? In the ensuing comparison the Republic came off second best. It was then only a step to the conclusion that the Republic was something detestable and that monarchy was far better. And, as far as I could see, there was nothing in the new Constitution or in the attitude of the public officials that might cause the people to change their minds. "We are lost," I said to myself, "without some miracle; the monarchists will not waste time in taking over."

I looked about me. I saw that many, many people were downhearted, yes, even many patriots were downhearted who earlier had waged so valiant and victorious a struggle for freedom. Demoralization had spread far and wide and an absolute paralysis of popular initiative had set in. The masses had been stripped of all basic guarantees against the excesses of their rulers, and so disarmed. Our brave revolutionaries still bore the marks of their ancient chains; not a few of them, who did not think the matter through very clearly, had almost come to the conclusion that the Republic could not be anything so marvelous after all. And so the people had fallen into a mood of surrender or something very close to it. Many seemed resigned and ready to go once more under the despot's yoke. I could see none who were ready to move forward, to rally the people, to fan to life again their revolutionary mood. The passion for freedom, I told myself, still burns in their hearts! Perhaps there is still time to save the Republic. Now is the time to muster our forces; I, for one, will not fail to play my part.

I launched the *Tribune of the People* and through it I spoke to the masses.

Listen to me, I say, *many of you have drawn the conclusion from the long succession of disasters which we have suffered that the Republic is worthless and that monarchy is to be preferred. You are right*—and I spell it out in capitals, for all to see—*WE WERE BETTER OFF UNDER THE BOURBONS THAN WE ARE NOW UNDER THE REPUBLIC. But,* I continue, *we must be clear which Republic we mean. We may concede that the Republic, as we have experienced it up to the present, is worthless. This, my friends, is not the real Republic. The real Republic is something of which we have not yet made trial. Let me try and explain it. I am almost certain that you will find it worth dying for.*

"Republic" is not just a word, a meaningless phrase. The slogan of liberty and equality, which was so long ago dinned into your ears, had a certain charm in the early days of the Revolution, because you believed that it contained real meaning. Today this slogan means nothing to you any more; it is only an empty oratorical flourish. But we must repeat again and again that this

MAXIMILIEN ROBESPIERRE

slogan, notwithstanding all our recent painful experiences, can and should connote something of deep significance for the masses.

The Revolution, I went on, ought not to pass into history as an event without meaning. It is inconceivable that the people should shed their blood in torrents only to end up in greater torment than before. When a nation takes the path of revolution it does so because the operation of evil institutions has brought society to such a pass that the majority of its members can no longer continue to exist in the old way. The masses realize that their situation is intolerable, they feel impelled to change it, and they are drawn into motion for that end. The people, in this case, do right to take a revolutionary path; the only reason for the institution of society in the first instance was to promote the happiness of the community. All of this is summed up in the slogan: the aim of society is the welfare of its members.

This slogan, I said, I took from the first article of the Constitution of the year I of the Republic; it has always been mine, and it always will be.

The aim of the Revolution, furthermore, is to realize the happiness of the majority. If, therefore, this aim is not fulfilled, if the people do not succeed in attaining the better life which was the object of their struggle, then the Revolution is not over. There may be those whose only concern is to substitute their own rule for that of monarchy, but it makes no difference what such people say or want. If the Revolution is brought to an end in mid-passage, it will be judged by history as little more than a catalogue of bloody crimes.

With this in mind I strove to make known the nature of the common welfare, which is the purpose of social existence, or the happiness of the greatest number, which is the purpose of the

Revolution. I pondered how it could be that at a given time the majority were worse off than they ought to be; and the conclusions that I reached I ventured to set forth in one of the first issues of the *Tribune* following 13 vendémiaire.

There are, I wrote, historical periods during which the final result of oppressive law is the appropriation of the bulk of social wealth by a minority. Social peace, natural when men are happy, then gives way to class war. The masses can no longer find a way to go on living; they see that they possess nothing and that they suffer under the harsh and flinty oppression of a greedy ruling class. The hour strikes for great and memorable revolutionary events, already foreseen in the writings of the times, when a general overthrow of the system of private property is inevitable, when the revolt of the poor against the rich becomes a necessity that can no longer be postponed.

I had also observed that the main actors on the revolutionary scene had realized before I did that the goal of the Revolution ought to be to redress the evil wrought by archaic and rotten social institutions, and to promote the happiness of the people. I had even gone so far as to assemble carefully the testimony on this score of one of our great legal theorists, who had died at the height of his powers.[5] The prosecution took the trouble to make an exhibit out of these mere notes, notwithstanding that they were obviously copied faithfully from well-known sources. This exhibit is number 71 in the second volume of the indictment. Since the whole piece was designed to be used against me, the court will doubtless allow me to quote part of it in my own defense:

Happiness is a new idea in Europe . . . Do not tolerate a single instance of poverty and misery in the State . . . Let Europe know that you will permit no more downtrodden people and no more

45

oppressors on French soil . . . It is the destiny of the wretched
of the earth to rule it; theirs is the right to talk as masters to the
governments that neglect them . . . Economic necessity alone
puts the toilers into the power of their enemies. Do you really
think that an empire can survive if political relationships are
shaped by those who are opposed to the existing form of gov-
ernment?

I reprinted these shafts of light in the *Tribune*. It was my aim
to make use of them to explain and illustrate to the people the
true objectives of the Revolution and the true nature of the
Republic. My readers' response was clear enough, I thought.
They were ready to embrace a Republic such as I described to
them. I dared to believe that my writings fired the people with
a desire to win a truly republican regime, and had not a little
to do with weaning the masses from their royalist sympathies.

"So far, so good," you will say, "but, really, you pushed your
ideas to extremes. . . ." This is a criticism that must now be
examined.

The prosecution has reproduced (page 78 of the appendix to
the indictment) a document entitled "Outline of Babeuf's Doctrine." This piece has been the subject of much debate in some
of the correspondence connected with this trial; and it has been
viewed as the most radical of all subversive doctrines. Let us
examine it further.

Nature, we read there, *has endowed every man with an equal*
right to the use of nature's gifts. The function of society is to
defend this equality of right from the unending attacks of those
who, in the state of nature, are wicked and strong; and to en-
hance, by collective action, collective happiness.

Nature has placed everyone under an obligation to work. None
may exempt himself from work without committing an anti-

social action. Work and its fruits should be common to all. Oppression exists when one man is ground down by toil and lacks the barest necessaries of life, while another revels in luxury and idleness. It is impossible for anyone, without committing a crime, to appropriate for his own exclusive use the fruits of the earth or of manufacture.

In a truly just social order there are neither rich nor poor. The rich, who refuse to give up their superfluous wealth for the benefit of the poor, are enemies of the people.

None may be permitted to monopolize the cultural resources of society and hence to deprive others of the education essential for their wellbeing. Education is a universal human right.

The purpose of the Revolution is to abolish inequality and to restore the common welfare. The Revolution is not yet at an end, since the wealthy have diverted its fruits, including political power, to their own exclusive use, while the poor in their toil and misery lead a life of actual slavery and count for nothing in the State.

I have pointed out, under cross-examination, that this document did not come from my pen, but that, since it was indeed a statement of the doctrines I had espoused, I gave it my approval and agreed to its being printed and published. This document was, in effect, a faithful summary of the ideas that I had set forth in the various issues of the *Tribune*.

These ideas, as it seems, constitute the central and fundamental evidence for the existence of the conspiracy that is charged against us. They are blazoned in the indictment under the heading "Confiscation of Private Property." The prosecution exploits them in order to arouse terror and disgust, resorting to the use of all sorts of odious and sensational epithets—agrarian revolution, piracy, havoc, anarchy, subversion of the social order,

chaos, unnatural plot, and what have you. It depicts the consequence of our advocacy as "the annihilation of the human species; the abandonment of the chance survivors to a condition of
utter savagery, to a primitive and skulking existence in the
bush; the destruction of civilization; the supremacy of the strong
over the weak; and the reduction of men to a condition more
bestial than that of the beasts themselves, quarreling fiercely
over scraps of fodder."

We have been brought here to defend ourselves against a
charge of conspiracy because of our ideas, and for no other reason. All the rest of the indictment is subordinate to this. The
man who wills an end also wills the means to gain that end. It
is immaterial whether you agree with the government and
brand the changes that we propose as subversion, or whether
you go along with the political scientists and think of them as a
sublime rebirth: it is clear that these changes cannot be achieved
without the overthrow of the existing government and without
measures to eliminate whatever obstacles stand in the way. This
overthrow of the established order, with whatever repressive
measures accompany it, is a necessary consequence of willing the
original goal. They are means ineluctably imposed upon those
who desire to achieve that goal, the establishment of what we
and the political theorists term "collective welfare" and what
the prosecution terms "havoc and plunder."

As we see, the central, and practically the sole charge against
us, is an alleged intent to set up a social system about which
there is a drastic difference of opinion. The other parts of the
indictment are only branches growing out of this main stem.

If this conclusion is correct, I must examine the following
questions: Have I really advocated the establishment of a new
social system? What type of advocacy have I undertaken? Was

LOUIS-ANTOINE DE SAINT-JUST

it a matter of theory and speculation, or did I really conspire to bring about my plans by main force and without the support of the people? Has the system that I advocate actually been proven to be evil and destructive? Am I the only one who has advocated it? Did no one advocate it before me? Were any steps taken, even under the Bourbons, to punish its supporters?

Some of these questions may be answered easily enough. As for the first, a few words suffice. I have indeed advocated the principles of collective happiness—that is, of the general welfare, the welfare of all. I have taught that the social philosophy which states, as a major premise, that the welfare of the people is *the sole objective of social organization,* has given expression to an irrefutable principle of truth and justice. I find it simply impossible to deny that men would ever have agreed to associate if they had foreseen that the consequences of such association would be unequivocally evil; if they had foreseen a state of affairs in which the masses were pressed down into a life of toil and hunger, and obliged, in blood and tears, to maintain a handful of privileged beings in idleness and profligacy. But if such a state of affairs does indeed come into existence, it is my right as a man, since man's eternal rights may never be alienated, to demand the restoration of the original social contract. Silent and unwritten though this contract may have been, nature has inscribed it ineradicably upon the human heart. Yes, there is a voice that cries out for all to hear: "The aim of society is the welfare of its members." That was the reason for the first social contract, and there was never need to spell it out at greater length—a single sentence suffices. All governments derive their authority from this great original source. They may not swerve in their dedication to it.

As for the second question—that of the type of advocacy I have

50

undertaken—I have set forth my ideas purely and simply to draw popular attention to a social philosophy. There was no question of these ideas being put into effect if the people willed otherwise. As a matter of fact, I was very far from enjoying any measure of popular support. He who thinks that such support is easy to win, fools himself. On the contrary, it is only too easy to become discouraged by the difficulties and the dangers involved in taking a case to the public, and only too tempting to conclude that the enterprise is hopeless before even putting the matter to the test.

In the course of my defense I shall proceed to prove that I have done nothing to put my ideas into effect by main force and in the absence of widespread popular support.

In order, gentlemen of the jury, to determine whether my ideas are, as the prosecution alleges, damnable, vicious, and subversive, you will need to take into account the contrary view of the matter that I have set forth in the course of my agitational work. I have myself prepared and published a summary of my ideas, and this I shall proceed to place before you. This will supplement the statement of my views that has already been entered in evidence, but which, I remind you, was not of my own composition, even though I gave it my apprôval. In the light of what currently passes for socially acceptable conduct, some of my notions may shock you a little. Withhold judgment, I beg you, and hear me out. You are called here to judge my innermost soul; and you must, therefore, plumb the aspirations that lie deepest in my heart, that have given meaning to my life. As I shall try to show you, the desire to be of service to mankind has animated all my thinking. This you may see from the frank confession of my political faith, which I consider it my duty to lay before you precisely as I have propagated it. In the *Tribune of the People* (number 35, page 102), I wrote:

Man's condition ought not to have deteriorated in passing from a state of nature to a state of social organization. In the beginning the soil belonged to none, its fruits to all. The introduction of private property was a piece of trickery put over on the simple and unsuspecting masses. The laws that buttressed property operated inevitably to create social classes—privileged and oppressed, masters and slaves.

The law of inheritance is a sovereign wrong. It breeds misery even from the second generation. Two sons of a rich man receive equal shares of their father's fortune. One son has but one child, the other, twelve. Of these twelve each receives only a twelfth part of the fortune of his uncle and the twenty-fourth part of the fortune of his grandfather. This portion is not enough to live on; and so twelve poor men must work for one rich one. Hence we find masters and servants among the grandchildren of a single man.

The law of alienability is no less unjust. This one man, already master over all the other grandchildren in the same line, pays what he will for the work that they must do for him. Their wages are insufficient to maintain life and they are obliged to sell their meager inheritance to their master. They become landless men; and if they have children of their own, these inherit nothing.

The gulf between rich and poor, rulers and ruled, proceeds from yet another cause, the difference in value and in price that arbitrary opinion attaches to the diverse products of toil and manufacture. Thus a watchmaker's working day has been valued twenty times higher than a ploughman's or laborer's. The wages of the watchmaker enable him to get possession of the inheritance of twenty ploughmen whom he is thus in a position to

GEORGES DANTON

expropriate, and enhance his own condition.

These three roots of our public woes—heredity, alienability, and the differing values which arbitrary opinion assigns to different types of social product—proceed from the institution of private property. All the evils of society flow from them. They isolate the people from each other; they convert every family into a private commonwealth, pit it against society at large, and dedicate it with an ever growing emphasis to inequality in all its vicious, suicidal forms.

I formulated these observations and came to think of them as self-evident truths. It did not take me very long to draw the following conclusions:

If the earth belongs to none and its fruits to all; if private ownership of public wealth is only the result of certain institutions that violate fundamental human rights; then it follows that this private ownership is a usurpation; and it further follows that all that a man takes of the land and its fruits beyond what is necessary for sustenance is theft from society.

And being drawn from one conclusion to another, believing as I did that no truth must be permitted to remain hidden from the minds of men, I became convinced of the truth of the following ideas, which I caused to be published:

All that a citizen lacks for the satisfaction of his various daily needs, he lacks because he has been deprived of a natural property right by the engrossers of the public domain. All that a citizen enjoys beyond what is necessary for the satisfaction of his daily needs he enjoys as a result of a theft from the other members of society. In this way a more or less numerous group of people is deprived of its rightful share in the public domain.

Inheritance and alienability are institutions destructive of basic human rights.

The plea of superior ability and industry is an empty rationalization to mask the machinations of those who conspire against human equality and happiness. It is ridiculous and unfair to lay claim to a higher wage for the man whose work requires more concentrated thought and more mental effort. Such effort in no way expands the capacity of the stomach. No wage can be defended over and above what is necessary for the satisfaction of a person's needs.

The worth of intelligence is only a matter of opinion, and it still remains to be determined if natural, physical strength is not of equal worth. Clever people have set a high value upon the creations of their minds; if the toilers had also had a hand in the ordering of things, they would doubtless have insisted that brawn is entitled to equal consideration with brain and that physical fatigue is no less real than mental fatigue.

If wages are not equalized, the clever and persevering are given a licence to rob and despoil with impunity those less fortunately endowed with natural gifts. In this way the economic equilibrium of society is upset, for nothing has been more conclusively proven than the maxim: a man only succeeds in becoming rich through the spoliation of others.

All our civic institutions, our social relationships, are nothing else but the expression of legalized barbarism and piracy, in which every man cheats and robs his neighbor. In its festering swamp our swindling society generates vice, crime, and misery of every kind. A handful of well-intentioned people band together and wage war on these evils, but their efforts are futile. They can make no headway because they do not tackle the problem at its roots, but apply palliatives based upon the distorted thinking of a sick society.

It is clear from the foregoing that whatever a man possesses over and above his rightful share of the social product has been stolen. It is therefore right and proper to take this wealth back again from those who have wrongfully appropriated it. Even a man who shows that he can do the work of four, and who consequently demands the wages of four, will still be an enemy of society; he is using criminal means to shake the social order and to obliterate its sacred equality. Common sense tells us, with no small emphasis, that we should curb a man of this type and drive him out as if he had the plague. At the very least he should be allowed to perform no more than one man's work and to lay claim to no more than one man's pay. The human species alone has made insane value distinctions between one of its members and another. As a result, the human species alone has been obliged to experience misery and want. There is no need for men to lack those things which nature has provided for all, though, of course, if want should arise as a result of the unavoidable calamities of wind, storm, flood, or famine, such privation must be borne and shared equally by all.

The creations of the human hand and mind become the property of society, part of the nation's capital, from the very moment that thinkers and workers bring these creations into being. Invention is the fruit of prior investigation and effort. The most recent workers in the field reap their reward as a result of the social labors of their predecessors in a society that nurtures invention and that aids the scientific worker in his task. It is clear that if knowledge is a social product it must be shared by all alike.

It is a truth, which only ignorant or prejudiced people are likely to contest, that if knowledge were made available to all alike, it would serve to make men roughly equal in ability and even in talent. Education is a monstrosity when it is unequally shared, since then it becomes the exclusive patrimony of a sec-

tion of society; it becomes, in the hands of this section, a set of tools, an ideological armory, with the help of which the privileged make war upon the defenseless masses. In this way the rich succeed, with little difficulty, in stifling and deceiving and robbing the people, thus subjecting them to a shameful servitude.

One thinker[6] expressed a profound truth when he wrote: "Talk as long as you will of the forms of government; it will all be idle speculation until you destroy the seeds of human greed and acquisitiveness." Society must be made to operate in such a way that it eradicates once and for all the desire of a man to become richer, or wiser, or more powerful than others.

Putting this more exactly, we must try to bring our fate under control, try to make the lot of every member of society independent of accidental circumstances, happy or unhappy. We must try to guarantee to each man and his posterity, however numerous, a sufficiency of the means of existence, and nothing more. We must try and close all possible avenues by which a man may acquire more than his fair share of the fruits of toil and the gifts of nature.

The only way to do this is to organize a communal regime which will suppress private property, set each to work at the skill or job he understands, require each to deposit the fruits of his labor in kind at the common store, and establish an agency for the distribution of basic necessities. This agency will maintain a complete list of people and of supplies, will distribute the latter with scrupulous fairness, and will deliver them to the home of each worker.

A system such as this has been proven practicable by actual experience, for it is used by our twelve armies with their 1,200,000 men. And what is possible on a small scale can also be done on a large one. A regime of this type alone can ensure the general

welfare, or, in other words, the permanent happiness of the peo-
ple—the true and proper object of organized society.

Such a regime, I continued, will sweep away iron bars, dun-
geon walls, and bolted doors, trials and disputations, murders,
thefts and crimes of every kind; it will sweep away the judges
and the judged, the jails and the gibbets—all the torments of
body and agony of soul that the injustice of life engenders; it
will sweep away enviousness and gnawing greed, pride and
deceit, the very catalogue of sins that Man is heir to; it will
remove—and how important is this!—the brooding, omnipres-
ent fear that gnaws always and in each of us concerning our fate
tomorrow, next month, next year, and in our old age; concern-
ing the fate of our children and of our children's children.

Such, gentlemen of the jury, was the body of truth that I concerned myself with and that I thought to have divined from my
study of the ageless book of nature. These were truths that I
did no more than discover and make known. I loved humanity;
and I was convinced that a social system such as I had conceived
alone would ensure the happiness of man. I was eager, therefore, to gain the attention of my fellows, to win them to my way
of thinking. But I was not so rash or presumptuous as to believe
that my task would be easy. In the present epoch men are dom-
inated and corrupted by a host of evil passions, so that it is not
difficult to see that the odds are more than 100 to 1 against the
realization of a project such as mine. Even the most impassioned
advocate of my ideas would not deny this.

As you see, gentlemen of the jury, I was seeking above all else
release from anguish of soul. When you love your fellow men and
think deeply about the woes of which they are at one and the same
time the victims and the authors, it is only natural to turn over in
your mind possible solutions for their plight. If a man feels that

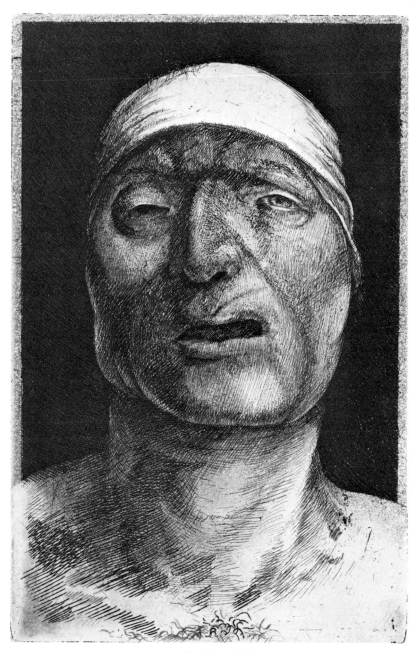

JEAN-PAUL MARAT

he has hit upon a remedy, but lacks the power to carry it into effect, he suffers on behalf of those whom, perforce, he must abandon to their misery; and he permits himself the faint relief of outlining the advantages of his scheme for the permanent abolition of human wretchedness. Such was the practice of our reformers and legal theorists whose mere disciple, popularizer, imitator, interpreter, and echo I was. As Rousseau said, "I understand well that one must not undertake the vain task of reforming mankind, but I have felt obliged to tell the whole truth as I have seen it." In condemning me, gentlemen of the jury, for the ideas which I have openly espoused and advocated, you place these great thinkers, my masters and guides, in the dock. My ideas are the same as theirs; it was in their pages that I studied those principles of "plunder" which the prosecution has branded as subversive. And you should also convict the Bourbons for their weak-kneed failure to prosecute subversion as relentlessly as the first Republic, and for their failure to put a stop to the circulation of the insidious writings of Mably, Helvetius, Diderot, Jean-Jacques Rousseau, and the rest.

These are the men whose philosophical poison has worked my ruin. But for them I would doubtless be blessed with the morality and the virtues of our modern philanthropists; I too would shudder at the thought of "looting" and the violent overthrow of the existing social order; like them, I would have the tenderest concern for the tiny minority of the rich and powerful; like them, I would have a heart devoid of pity for the suffering masses. But, gentlemen, there is no danger of my joining your company; I shall never live to repent the day that I learned my lessons at the feet of those masters whose illustrious names I have just mentioned. I shall not denounce them and I shall not recant the heresies that they have taught me. Let the ax fall, for

I am ready. There is no better way for a man to die than to offer his life for the sake of justice.

The prosecution has drawn up an indictment of our democratic and popular ideas which it has labelled "conspiracy for the confiscation of private property." If, gentlemen of the jury, you find us guilty of such a conspiracy, it is literally true to say, as I have said, that all the great thinkers whose ashes rest in the Pantheon will stand convicted with us here. These thinkers conceived plans very similar to ours and undertook to make them known. Excerpts from their writings have been reproduced in the indictment, and this gives me grounds to believe that they are on trial here with us. What are the quotations from Rousseau, that I shall cite later, doing here, if the intention is not to convict him along with us? There are also others, reproduced on pages 74 to 76 of the indictment, and I quote (II, 74):

Before the frightful words mine *and* thine *were invented; before the existence of that brutal and cruel class of men called* masters *and of that other class of lying rogues called* slaves; *before the appearance of men so wicked that they* dared to have too much whilst others were starving; *before a reciprocal dependence forced all to become deceivers, informers, and traitors; before all this was, what crimes and vices, I should like to know, could men have had? Tell me that men have long since abandoned the Golden Age: as well tell me that they have long since given up the ideal of the Good Life!*

The draft of this document, we are told, is in Babeuf's hand. But I tell you that it is only a copy. The proof that I shall offer for this quotation you will accept, I trust, for the others too. The original words came from the pen of Jean-Jacques Rousseau. A new conspirator is added to our company, but I am not afraid to compromise him; he is beyond the power of this Court to pillory or punish. I make no bones about the fact that Rousseau was the guiding spirit behind the *Société des Démocrates* of floréal. The words that I have just quoted, he wrote in 1758 in the course of his correspondence with M. Bordes, an academician of Lyon, in connection with the *Discourse on the Arts and Sciences*.[7] His statement, as we see, was made long before the conspiracy now under investigation. But what difference does that make? Clearly the conspiracy is much older than the prosecution dreamed. Poor Jean-Jacques! This will not save you from being sentenced *in absentia*, along with Félix Le Peletier, Robert Lindet, and Drouet!! It is lucky indeed, as I have said, that you are beyond the reach of this Court.

To proceed. At the bottom of page 75 I read:

What would the human race be like if it were composed of workers, soldiers, hunters, and shepherds? A wise man will sooner seek happiness among these, the common people, than virtue among the cooks, poets, painters, goldsmiths, printers, and musicians who compose the balance of humanity.

Rousseau wrote these words in the very same letter to academician Bordes that I have just referred to. One must admit that his thoughts have much in common with those of the floréal conspirators. Take the following slogan from the *Manifeste des Égaux*,[8] which the prosecution quotes with such care: "Let the arts perish, if need be, so long as we retain true equality." This phrase is an echo of Rousseau pure and simple; as we see, it is not for nothing that Rousseau's ideas have been included in the indictment. I say again that this draft is none of mine, nor are its concluding statements, which I proceed to read (page 76):

People think to embarrass me greatly by asking me: At what point do you draw the line in regard to the use of luxuries? I answer that all luxury is superfluous—everything is superfluous

above and beyond the sheerest of physical necessities. Every-
thing beyond this is a source of evil.

This is pure heresy, every bit as radical as "let the arts perish."
But what follows modifies it a little:

I am not suggesting that men be compelled to be satisfied
with basic necessities and I know that it is silly to think of
changing human nature by such a course of action. I do but
observe the evil effects of luxury and try to trace the causes.
Let those who are bolder or wiser than I suggest the remedies.

As you may easily see, it is writers like Rousseau who have
subverted us. But what about M. Bordes of Lyon, who was the
recipient of the letters that contained these doctrines? Is he still
alive and what did he think of it all? I think that I can call to
mind his answers to Rousseau: he did not share at all the latter's
subversive ideas.

Gentlemen of the jury, I must needs offer you the most rigor-
ous proof in order to convince you that the beliefs of which we
are accused, the ideas which have been the occasion for so loud
an outcry against us, are simply the beliefs and the ideas of
teachers of mankind who command the respect of everyone. The
authority of these eminent men must, in the last analysis, carry
some weight. If we can prove that we have merely popularized
under the Republic the selfsame truths which they freely entertained and made known under the old regime, perhaps you
will stop thinking of us as dangerous and radical innovators, fit
for nothing but the gallows.

Rousseau, who is cast here in the role of our accomplice, has
written little on this topic over and above what I have already
cited. But a few words of Rousseau's speak volumes. I remem-
ber, still, these terse, sublime sentences of his:

The progress of society depends upon all having enough and none too much—You are lost if you forget that the fruits of the earth belong to all, the earth itself to none—Are you ignorant of the fact that millions of your fellow creatures suffer the pangs of want and perish for lack of those things that you have too much of? And do you not know that you ought to obtain the express and unanimous consent of the human race before taking a larger share of the community's wealth than is rightfully yours? —Notwithstanding all the efforts of the wisest lawmakers, the body politic has remained defective because it has been the product of haphazard growth. Time might reveal faults and suggest remedies, but a constitution defective from the beginning can never be repaired. Instead of sweeping away the old, clearing the air, and making a fresh start, as Lycurgus did in Sparta, there has been endless patching and improvisation. The all-consuming fires of ambition, the lust to make one's fortune, not in order to satisfy a genuine need, but out of an insane frenzy to get ahead of others—this imparts to men an evil inclination for mutual destruction; it endows them with a secret hatred, all the more vile since it assumes a mask of benevolence in order to strike more effectively. We see, in a word, competition and rivalry here and everywhere, an everlasting collision of interests, a bottomless thirst to profit at the expense of others. All these evils are the first result and the inseparable accompaniment of private property. Where there is no private property there can be no wrong.

Such are the ravings of Rousseau, our co-conspirator, about private property which, the prosecution tells us, is "the foundation of the social order (page 67)." If the Genevan dreamer were still alive, he would learn soon enough that dissent is dangerous. Listen to the lesson that the prosecution would read him:

Destruction of the right to private property is bloody revolu-

ANACHARSIS CLOOTS

tion! Without private property, what would happen to industry and the arts? If the earth belongs to no one, who is to cultivate it? Who will glean its fruits, if none can say: they are mine? *Armed robbery will stalk the barren land. Social distinctions and privileges will be gone, but natural inequalities will remain. Men, grown through need more savage than beasts, will fight with fang and claw for scraps of food: for how can there be enough for a numerous population when industry and commerce no longer supplement what nature yields of itself? The extinction of the human race, with the last lone survivors wandering as savages in the wilderness—such is the perspective presented to us by the advocates of Babouvism (pages 67, 68).*

Bravo! You have been put to rout, Rousseau! Your famous *Discourse upon Inequality* has been refuted. Would it, I wonder, have carried away the prize at the Academy of Dijon, if the profound thinker who drew up the indictment of the floréal conspiracy had been among the judges?[9] Alas, if that literary competition had taken place in this land of freedom today, Rousseau would have been barred even from entering it! He would have been reported to the police, a warrant would have been issued for his arrest, an indictment would have been drawn —and he would have found himself sitting in the box here with the rest of the defendants.

And Mably—how would it have been with him? Mably, popular, humane, and sensitive, was much more of a radical than Rousseau, a conspirator of quite a different hue. His attack on private property followed different lines, and we must pay attention to him too. Then we shall have to decide if it is edifying to see the Republic proceeding against the disciples when, under the Capets, the masters freely and loudly professed the selfsame doctrines.

Nature, says Mably, *decrees equality in the wealth and condition of the people as a law of the welfare of states....*

Elsewhere he writes:

The lawmaker does his work in vain if he does not, in the first instance, concern himself with establishing equality in the wealth and condition of the people.... Trace back, says he further on, *our difficulties to their source. You will find them linked at the start to inequality of wealth.*

He returns to the theory of the State and of natural law, saying:

Equality is necessary for men. Nature gave it as a law to our earliest ancestors. She declared her intentions so unequivocally that it was impossible to be ignorant of them. Who can deny that when we enter the world we enjoy the most perfect equality? Does not nature endow all men with the same organs, the same needs, the same reason? Are not the fruits of the earth put there for the common enjoyment of all mankind? Where, may I ask, do you find a law of inequality? Did nature set aside for each man a patrimony of his own? Did she place markers in the fields? And did she make some men rich and others poor?

Our philosopher dreams himself back through the ages, and speculates about the establishment of the first social systems. Here is his idea of what happened:

It seems reasonable to assume, he says, *that our forefathers, obliged to labor in order to live, pooled their forces, just as they had previously combined together to set up a public authority. They sowed together and so they would reap. You see with what wisdom nature contrived to bring us to the enjoyment of a collective way of life and to prevent us from falling into the abyss of private property. As far as I am concerned, collectivity is no wild dream; on the contrary, I find it hard to conceive how on earth humanity blundered into private ownership of goods.*

He proceeds to develop the principles in accordance with which the collective society is to be planned; and he is lost in admiration of the simplicity and happiness that result:

I believe, he exclaims with delight, *that the people are to be divided into different categories; the strongest are assigned to till the soil, the others to perform other essential tasks. Everywhere there will be public storehouses where the products of labor will be deposited. The magistrates, true fathers of the Republic, will have almost no other function but to safeguard morals and to distribute the necessaries of life to each family.*

Elsewhere, after stating that private property is the main source of the misfortunes that afflict mankind, Mably attacks the vicious system of inheritance.

No matter, he writes, *how equally the wealth of a Republic is originally divided, we may be certain that by the third generation this equality will be no more. You, for example, have an only son, brought up under your supervision to a life of hard work and thrift. He will be the sole heir to a carefully managed fortune. I, less energetic, less talented, less industrious, or less lucky, will have to divide my savings between three or four lazy or spendthrift children. These people are of necessity unequal, since inequality of wealth generates inevitably different needs and a kind of slavery that has nothing in common with the laws of nature and of reason.*

Discussing, finally, the plan of his projected commonwealth, Mably says:

It will be composed of all in complete equality—all rich, all poor, all free, all brothers. The first law will be a ban on private property. We will deposit the fruits of our toil in the public stores. This will be the wealth of the State and the property of all. Every year the heads of families will elect stewards whose task will be the distribution of goods to each in accordance with his needs, the allotment of tasks to be performed by each, and the maintenance of public order.

I will single out for special mention that part of the indictment of 6 ventôse that takes upon itself to frame an answer to these and similar speculations. On page 67 of the indictment I find a paragraph which, it seems to me, was specifically intended as an answer to Mably the democrat. Mably based himself on reason and principle. It suffices, it seems, to make a reply with mere windy oratory:

The chasm yawns, immeasurable to man. What tongue can tell the dire effect when the fearsome proletarian mob, spawned by debauch, by idleness, by the gamut of lewd vices that breed in a corrupted people, hurls itself in a single bound upon the property owners, these wise, farsighted, hard-working men who form the very backbone of the nation?

How easy it is for rulers, backed by the power of the state, to overthrow with a few foolish words an entire system based upon reason and logic! It matters nothing that Mably was a highly educated man, that he bore the stamp of genius and a family name rightly renowned. The nation has been offered insults in this Court which I am in no position to avenge. The officials of the *ancien regime* itself would scarcely have dared to go so far in their expressions of disdain for the people. We agree, at least, that the mass of the propertyless, the proletarians, is "frightening," that it constitutes the majority of "a corrupted people," that the sole exception is a class of "wise and farsighted property owners," whose interests alone politicians and lawyers deem it an honor to serve. As for the masses, "spawned by debauch, by idleness, by the gamut of lewd vices," these amount to less than nothing. That the masses toil and that they are under

69

the absolute domination of the "wise, farsighted, hard-working" minority—this, evidently, is of no importance at all.

Has it not occurred to you, gentlemen of the jury, that our poor scribblings about equality and communal system are only echoes of, commentaries upon, the great thinkers who have pondered these things long before ourselves? Is it not idle to believe that we could make a more powerful impact upon the public mind than they? Their works, so justly famed, are available to all in new and modern editions, but no one is afraid that this will in itself precipitate a revolution against private property. What need then to worry about our ideas, whose currency is so much more restricted and which are much less capable of producing an impression upon people? The *Manifeste des Égaux* has been gathering dust on the shelf and perhaps would never have won the least attention without the publicity which this Court has so kindly given it. It certainly contains no other ideas than the manifestoes of Mably and Rousseau that I have been discussing. Why then so much fuss about it? You, men of property, have no fear of us! Rely upon the passions, vices, prejudices, and customs that dominate the people for the maintenance of your beloved social system. Ambition, greed, and egotism are the barriers that will keep you from harm. I will not insult our people by asserting that they are totally "corrupted," but I do say that they have not strength enough to establish a social order which, if the testimony of wise men is to be believed, would bring them happiness —pure, natural, simple, innocent happiness, happiness of which they are so completely deprived that they cannot even conceive it.

I have been accused of a revolutionary advocacy of equality and I have been branded as an organizer of "looting." It remains for me to cite one more eminent authority in my defense. This is none other than Diderot, the most determined, bold, and, I

LAZARE CARNOT

might almost say, passionate champion of the communal system. I shall try and show that he battled on its behalf more valiantly than we, and that kings permitted him to do so. In this way I shall perhaps succeed in allaying the hysteria that the prosecution has sought to foster by insisting that the mere mention of the words "collective happiness" in a pamphlet was enough to bring about the overthrow of the system of private property.

Political philosophers always go back to natural law in order to ascertain the true basis of popular rights. If their intentions are honest they will strive to follow natural law faithfully; they will, in no single detail, discard nature's design, for this has been expressed so clearly and unequivocally that an honest man has no difficulty in grasping it. Among the best of such interpreters of nature was Diderot.[10] Here are the lessons that he has left to us from his scrutiny of her sacred book:

Nature, he exclaims, *has impressed upon men, by means of their common human needs and human feelings, their equality in fact and in right, and the necessity for a collective life.*

The only vice that I can see in the universe is human greed. *Any others that you might mention are mere aspects or forms of this, the mother of vices. Look closely at vanity, self-love, pride, ambition, deceit, hypocrisy, villainy; even sift carefully the majority of our fashionable virtues and you will find at bottom that subtle and pernicious passion,* greed. *Action that seems disinterested often only masks it. No one, I believe, will debate the self-evident truth that if you abolish private property you will also abolish the evils which it generates.*

Diderot goes on to debate the reason why human laws are bad. He finds it in the fact that laws are based upon faulty first premises. All the authors of effective reform plans grapple with the same ideas, and even use the very same expressions, because they all proceed from the same first principles. He explains and defines the fundamental weakness of constitutional codes, and says:

In the matter of legislative reform it is better to leave alone what is bad than to meddle without achieving any improvement. Laws which have provided only palliatives for the sufferings of humanity are the direct cause of the evil results of their bungling approach. Such laws, too, are indirectly to blame for the evils which they intensify or fail to eliminate. Reformers have too often confused good and bad, and have labored, so to say, to perfect and to systematize imperfection itself.

What is the practical bearing of all this? Diderot is trying to show that legislation will not have the value of the paper it is written upon if it does not take, as its first premise, the abolition of private property. Here is his conclusion:

The one and only reason, he says, for the evil and disordered state of society lies in the obstinacy of lawmakers who insist on breaking or causing to be broken the primary and essential bond of social existence, by giving continued sanction to the private ownership of wealth filched from the domain that by right belongs to all mankind.

Diderot examines this idea from many points of view. In one place he writes:

From the royal scepter to the shepherd's crook, from the tiara to the monkish cowl, the mainspring of human action is no mystery: it is personal interest. And what gave birth to this monster of selfishness? Private property! You, learned people, who amuse yourselves with discussions about the best form of government, you may wag your jaws till doomsday; all your civic wisdom will not improve the condition of man by one hair's breadth if you do not lay the ax to the tree of private ownership.

At another place he expresses the same idea with a broad sweep, in one simple sentence: "Would the rise and fall of empires," he asks, "ever be possible in a world where all property was held in common?"[11]

Elsewhere the philosopher views the matter from the standpoint of the profound ignorance that exists among men and that is generated by the absence of his favored system.

Precisely when, he asks, *did the masses become a blind herd? Can we not trace this to the introduction of private property and self-interest? These, with the delusions that are their consequence, have generated such a complex of conflicting wills that you will hardly find ten people out of a thousand who are able to agree either upon a common aim or upon the proper way to go about achieving it. Almost no one has any idea of what constitutes the essence of the truly good in human association, no matter how tiny the group that is being considered.*

Elsewhere, again, Diderot considers the matter in relation to the abolition of crime and injustice:

While natural law is fully operative, crime is unthinkable. If man is free of the tyranny of private property, it is quite impossible for him to be a wrongdoer, a thief, a murderer, or a marauder. Abolish private property and its attendant evils and men will not need to arm themselves for attack or defense. There will be an end to savage passions and savage deeds, an end to evil thoughts and evil plans. Private property and selfishness drive men on to sacrifice the human race itself upon the altar of private greed....

Our philosopher, naturally enough, draws precisely opposite conclusions from the concept of the collective ownership of wealth. He notes that everywhere in the world the most merciful and humane peoples have been those who have had little or no knowledge of private property, or those, at any rate, amongst whom the institution was least firmly rooted. As he goes on, our seer is carried away by his excitement. Imagination gives him wings and he dreams himself back to those far-off happy days when equality flourished in the world. "Nearly all peoples," he writes, with genuine delight, "have had, and retain to this very day, the memory of a Golden Age when there reigned among men that true and perfect equality whose principles I have been expounding."

Diderot then expresses regret that almost all the lawgivers in human history have failed to grasp and to formulate the true principles of social legislation:

When the peoples, weary of their own transgressions, began to yearn for the blessings of a truly collective existence and began to heed the advice and the leadership of men whom they deemed capable of reestablishing it, how easy would it then have been to teach men to know and to hate the ultimate cause of all their woes—private property!

He renews his complaints about the stupidity and the inadequacy of our ideas concerning the proper basis of law. "Our commentaries on the principles of social legislation," he writes sadly, "could have this subtitle: *How to civilize men by laws designed to make them fierce as tigers.*" He insists that private ownership lies at the root of war, both civil and international. Root out this plant and its evil flowers will wither. "The laws of war," he says, "are the laws of an armed truce. This has nothing to do with us. Rather put an end to war by destroying the thing that breeds it."

In a couple of words he depicts the bliss of the Golden Age, which has kindled in him so passionate an enthusiasm, and he says, "Laws worthy of the name ought to promote among the people so deep a feeling of brotherhood that none should stand in need, not only of what is necessary and useful, but even of what is pleasing."

Diderot permitted himself the hope that one day his exhortations would have their effect and that the people would finally be persuaded to carry out his plan. "I have indicated," he said, "the blow that must be struck at the root of all evil. *Men more able than myself will, I hope, one day succeed in convincing the people to take this step.*" Indeed, such was his faith, that he was perfectly confident that kings themselves would turn philosopher and adopt his ideas:

You mortals, he says, *whose destiny it is to rule nations, would you like to earn the thanks of a grateful people by founding the sublimest and most perfect of governments? START BY GIVING FULL ENCOURAGEMENT TO THE TRULY WISE MEN WHO ATTACK THE ERRORS AND PREJUDICES THAT MAINTAIN THE SYSTEM OF PRIVATE PROPERTY; IT WILL NOT TAKE LONG FOR YOU TO WIN THE ACCEPTANCE BY YOUR SUBJECTS OF LAWS VERY SIMILAR TO THOSE I HAVE SET FORTH AS LIKELY, IN ACCORDANCE WITH THE PROMPTINGS OF REASON, TO PROVE BEST FOR MEN.*

Diderot, in conclusion, deals with objections to his plans on the score of impracticability:

The practical difficulties, he assures us, *involved in putting into effect the laws on the allocation of jobs, public services, and the fair and orderly distribution of goods, are very minor. All this adds up to a simple problem of listing* things *and* people; *a matter, therefore, of simple mathematical calculation, it admits of easy solution. Social planners, both ancient and modern, have conceived and carried into effect projects of incomparably greater difficulty; and they have had to contend not merely with unforeseen complications, but with accidents of nature and with numberless obstacles arising from ignorance and error. It is amazing*

FILIPPO MICHELE BUONARROTI

that these rash people accomplished as much as they did.

Our philosopher then sets forth a complete legislative code formulated in accordance with the concepts of equality and of natural law as he interprets them. I reproduce below a selection of articles from this remarkable code:

I, Art. 1: A man shall have the right to own individually and as private property only those things that he is putting to effective use, either to satisfy his needs, or for his pleasure, or as the tools of his trade.

Art. 2: Every citizen shall be a public servant, employed and maintained at public expense.

Art. 3: Every citizen shall make his contribution to the State in accordance with his strength, ability, and age.

XV, Art. 1: Whosoever shall seek, either by plot or any other manner, to abolish the laws and to introduce the odious institution of private property, shall be imprisoned as a mad dog and an enemy of humankind.

Nothwithstanding the gravity of the subject and of my position here, I cannot refrain from drawing your attention to the irony of these words. The very same epithet, *mad dog,* which the prosecution hurls at those who conspire *for* equality, is used by Diderot to denote those who conspire *against* it.

I think that you will agree with me, gentlemen of the jury, that this dream of Diderot's is a far more finished affair than any of the speculations attributed to us. You must realize that in the matter of doctrine we are in reality no more than grade school students, mere disciples of the masters whose works I have here set forth. By "we," of course, I mean those of us who have concerned ourselves with philosophical matters, as shown by the documents that you have examined; I mean those of us who have applied our minds to the ideal construction of an egalitarian social system. How, then, was our achievement in any way comparable to Diderot's? What speculations have we been guilty of that in boldness and provocativeness could even begin to rival his, or Mably's, or Jean-Jacques Rousseau's? This *Manifeste des Égaux,* this so-called *analysis of the doctrine of Babeuf,* these tirades of the *Tribune,* these are mere pallid paraphrases of our three great philosophers and lawmakers. Since, under our republican form of government, there has never been any inquisition with power to suppress these books, how then can it be forbidden to explain and comment upon them? Has such commentary, in actuality, been forbidden? Of course not! The government does not dare to level an attack on the memory of our great thinkers, and so it attacks the commentators, the interpreters, and the disciples instead. What law entitles it to do this? There is none. We are still told that we have freedom of the press and freedom of thought. In public our rulers still make a formal bow to these democratic principles, but secretly they trample on them without blush or shame. Brute force usurps the place of right. Selfish interest has grasped the power of the state and it uses that power to bend principle and law itself to private ends. As I shall prove to you, I have been rotting in jail for a year solely on account of the use which I have dared to make of the right of freedom of the press and of thought.

Let us not lose sight of the powerful effect that Diderot's incisive words have surely produced in this Court on the most zealous champions of private property. There is in Diderot's words a peculiar power and brilliance that must assuredly have greatly diminished the impression created by the feeble writings of the floréal conspirators. The prosecution's shafts, one would think, are directed not so much against these latter-day alleged conspirators as against the author of the *Code de la Nature.* It is Diderot who must appear, in the eyes of our accusers, as the arch-conspirator. On his head the full force of their attack should fall. He is the man they should be addressing when they say:

Such is the collective happiness which these comrades, these egalitarians, are preparing for us. The mind recoils in horror when it contemplates the howling wilderness into which these fanatics would lead us. It stands appalled at the ghastly sights that line the road which they would have us tread. These monsters are ready to lead us through a bloody shambles to the destruction of civilization itself. When the roaring flames have consumed an entire city, nothing will be left, only a handful of survivors wandering in a daze amidst the smoking wreckage; while in their nearby lairs these villains will gloatingly divide up their loot—loot snatched from the bonfire that they themselves did kindle.

What strangely conflicting opinions men entertain! This is a black and dismal picture, a very supplement to Arthur Young. Look at the same picture through the eyes of Mably and Diderot: it is gay and beautiful, it is the Golden Age. Flowering and fruitful happiness, innocence, and justice are seen in the place of smoking ruins, corpses, tombs, and pirate lairs.

The indictment against me has attributed to me exclusive advocacy of certain subversive ideas. I have, I hope, diminished the hostility of public reaction if I have been able to show that our modern philosophers share with me this crime. But, further than this, I should point out to you that in quite recent years I have had, not co-propagandists, but many precursors who in their time seemed no less fervent in their advocacy than I. By producing a certain amount of evidence to prove that in all this I was in no sense an innovator, I shall perhaps be successful in correcting those people who up till now have seen in me an extraordinary and obviously very guilty man. These precursors of whom I now propose to speak are Tallien and Armand de la Meuse. If I show that I have said nothing more radical than they on this question of equality, I shall have to ask why I have been dragged before a court of justice, whereas they have not?

Tallien wrote the following, in February 1793, in his paper *The Workingman's Friend*, number 71:

There is much talk about anarchy. My feeling is that anarchy will vanish the moment that republican officials stop hatching plots against freedom. My feeling is that anarchy will vanish the moment that the gulf between the rich and the poor is diminished. *To put an end to misery through the confiscation of excessive riches, this is the inner purpose of the Revolution.*

Armand de la Meuse, speaking on the floor of the Convention, said on April 17, 1793:

Honest men will admit that next to winning equal rights before the law, the most natural and burning need is for social and economic equality. Equal rights before the law are only a cruel deception unless they are to constitute a stepping-stone to this higher social goal. Without this, equal rights will not guarantee happiness. They will only inflict upon honest, hard-working people the tortures of Tantalus. Primitive societies, let me add, cannot even have had any other goal than the establishment of the fullest practical equality among their members; and there cannot be, in my belief, a more dangerous, absurd, and immoral contradiction than political equality without social and economic equality. To enjoy equality in law but to be deprived of it in life is an odious injustice.

These metaphysical distinctions, the pompous products of egotistical display, are not for you. It is an eternal truth that equal rights, the rights of man, are a gift of nature, not a benefit con-

ferred by society. All of us must recognize this fact and take it into account or we shall learn it, painfully and late, in the hard school of experience. These equal rights have been violated in the state of nature. Man has frequently been too weak, with their aid alone, to achieve that real equality in the absence of which, equality of rights is a purely formal concept. For this reason men have joined together so that through collective action they may win social rights, the rights of the citizen.

If men, in a state of nature, are born equal in rights, they are definitely not born equal in their actual life situations. The brute force and the instinct which they possess in this state establish between one man and another a wide de facto *inequality, notwithstanding the formal equality of rights. Society and the institutions that flow from it cannot and ought not to have any other object than the achievement in life itself of the rights of man, by protecting the weak from the oppression of the strong and by placing the labor of the individual at the disposal of society itself.*

The most dangerous and cruel mistake which the Constituent and Legislative Assemblies and the National Convention may be said to have committed is that they followed slavishly in the footsteps of the lawmakers who went before them, that they failed to set limits to the unbridled rights of property, that they abandoned the people to the speculations of the heartless, money-grabbing rich.

There is no need to raise the question here as to whether natural law makes provision for property owners and whether under it all men possess an equal right to the fruits of the earth. This is a truth about which we can entertain no doubts at all. The real issue is this: granted that in society the public convenience admits of a right to private property, is there not also

AUGUSTIN-ALEXANDRE DARTHE

an obligation to limit those rights and not to abandon their use to the caprice of the property owner? If you assert that these rights are absolute, then the man who in the state of nature was exposed by virtue of his weakness to the oppression of the strong will, by entering into social relationships, only have exchanged one misfortune for another. What was weakness in the state of nature, in society is turned into poverty. Exploitation by the strong is changed to exploitation by schemers and by men of wealth. In this case society, so far from being a blessing to men, on the contrary, takes away their natural rights, and so adds insult to injury. For in the state of nature a man at least is free to fight the wild beasts for his food, while society, more ferocious than the beasts, has taken away this right by virtue of the social bond itself. It is hard to decide which is more amazing, the blind heartlessness of the rich or the long-suffering patience of the poor.

And yet the social order is based upon that long-suffering, all-forgiving patience which enables the idle rich to live in peace. Because of it, from his earliest days, the poor man bends in toil over the earth, finding relief only in the grave, when death has put an end to his suffering. And, as a reward for this, we propose to abandon the poor even more completely to the mercy of our barbarous institutions! We would dare to make perpetual the miseries and abuses that flow from them!

It is meaningless to argue that the poor and the rich enjoy the same equality in the eyes of the law. This is sophistry. Spiritual equality will not help a man who is starving or in want. Such equality, let me repeat, is the gift of nature and not of society— no man needs to enter the social state just for this. Far better for him if he had remained in the natural state, ranging the woods and the shores in search of his food and livelihood.

The first and most insidious objection to social and economic equality, and the most immoral, is based on the alleged right to private property, in the accepted sense of that word. What exactly is this right? Does it imply an unlimited power to do what one wants with one's own? If that is indeed what is meant, I say openly, it is nothing more or less than a return to the law of the jungle. It nullifies the purpose of society, it invites men to take the law into their own hands, it risks the dissolution of the body politic. But if that is not what is meant, then I ask, precisely what bounds are to be set to the exercise of this right? Some limits, presumably, must be set. You are not, surely, going to leave the matter up to the property owner's own sense of what is right?

Do you really want to secure the people's happiness? Do you want to make them contented? Do you want to give them a stake in the triumph of the Revolution and the stability of the Republic? Do you want to put an end to our domestic disturbances? Then make it known today that the basis of the republican constitution of the French People will be the limitation of property rights.

It is now no longer a question of making a revolution in men's minds; this is not the area where we should anticipate further success. This aspect of the work has already been carried through successfully, as all France knows. Now it is up to us to make a revolution in the realm of things, *for the future of the human race depends on this. Indeed, what is the use of a mere change of mind which wins for the masses only the dream of happiness? This change of mind is, no doubt, a fine thing, but such an ecstasy is proper only for clever people and for the favored children of fortune. It costs such people nothing to rave about liberty and equality. The masses, too, have been enraptured by the first breath of freedom. But beware: this intoxication will pass. Facing their condition with sober senses and finding it even more wretched than before, the masses will blame their raptures on the wiles of rabble-rousers and conclude that they have been made the sport of the lusts and ambitions of a scheming few. True happiness for the masses is today only a beautiful dream, not a reality. It cannot be realized without carrying through the revolution in things that has already been accomplished in* men's minds.

There, gentlemen of the jury, you have the doctrine expounded before the Convention by a man who is still a member of the present legislative body, a man whom no one has ever dreamed of calling a conspirator.

If I wished to rummage in the pages of ancient history, I would find other people of similar convictions. But I shall not do this. I shall limit myself to citing the example of the founder of the Christian religion. Nothing could be more specific than his words: *Love your brother as yourself; Do unto others as ye would that they do unto you.* That is, wish that others should be as happy as you wish to be, that they should be in all things equal with you, neither more nor less than you. It is true, of course, that when Jesus spread His message of human equality, he too was treated as the ringleader of a conspiracy.

CONCLUDING REMARKS

If our death is resolved upon; if the clock has struck and my time has come, the end will not find me unprepared. I have paid, since the very first days of the Revolution, a harsh penalty for my love of the people. Passing my life in the dungeon, I have been no stranger to the agony and the violent death that are, too often, inseparable from the revolutionary's lot. Death will not take me by surprise! For a whole year now I have lived upon the

Tarpeian rock. It has no terrors for me. On the contrary, I find it good to have my name set down upon the roll of those who have laid down their lives for love of their people. And certain I am that my name shall be upon that list! Count yourself, Gracchus Babeuf, among the most blessed of mortals, since you perish in the cause of justice.

All in all, there is much to console me at this hour. How could I hope for a more glorious end to my career? Before the final agony I shall have been granted a triumph that falls but rarely to those who give their lives for mankind. Almost without exception tyranny succeeds in stifling the truth along with the martyr who dies for the truth. Contemporaries, deceived or terrorized by the ruling power, only pour the searing acid of calumny and insult into the victim's gashes; and thus his agony is intensified a thousandfold. In the very presence of the wrongs committed by the deluded mob and its crafty misleaders, the martyr —who knows?—is far from feeling the consoling certainty that avenging time will redeem his reputation, summon all posterity to do him honor, and make certain his title to immortality. But we are more fortunate—we do not have to await the judgment of posterity! Tyranny has long been able to oppress us, but it has had no power to besmirch our names. Even in our own lifetime we have seen how the truth will out. Every pen records the facts that redound to our honor and that lock our tormentors in an eternal pillory. Yes, our very enemies, at least those who are not the most hostile to our opinions, have rendered us honor as honorable men. How much more certain, then, may we be that evenhanded history will deal justly with our memory. I bequeath to the future a written heritage. Every line of it shall testify that I lived and drew my breath only for one cause, the emancipation of the people.

And who are these men in whose midst I am delivered over to death? Drouet and Le Peletier, whose names are so dear to the Republic, these are my accomplices! And you, my friends, who surround me on these benches, who are you? Almost all of you are the founders and the most loyal supporters of the Republic. If the guillotine falls it will claim the last of the French patriots, the last of the republican vanguard. Royalist terror, which has already destroyed our comrades, will emerge triumphant with our destruction. Royalist steel will flash again to gather in a harvest of death among the ranks of the friends of freedom. Better, far better, that we should not witness these final scenes of disaster; better that we should die on our feet rather than live on our knees,[12] that we should sacrifice our lives gloriously because we wished to save the lives of others. Well may our end be eased by so sweet a consolation.

There is a further comfort. Is it not a source of joy to us that our wives and children have followed us here? Vulgar prejudice does not touch us: our dear ones have not blushed to follow us to this place where we sit at the very feet of the judges. The deeds that have brought us before this Court can cause neither them nor us to bow our heads in shame. Our dear ones will follow us to the very foot of Calvary to receive our blessing and our last farewell.

But oh, my children! I may not take you apart and talk to you alone, for this, my right and privilege as a father, has been denied me; and so I must speak to you from the courtroom bench where now I sit. I have only one thing to make known to you, one bitter regret. I wished, passionately, to do my part in the struggle to bequeath to you freedom, the source of all man's blessings; but I see that slavery will live on after me, that at my death I shall leave you in the grip of evil. I have nothing, nothing at all to bequeath to you!! I have no wish to pass on to you my love of justice, my deep hatred of tyranny, my dedication to the cause of equality and freedom, my bright love for the people. These gifts would be too deadly: of what use would they be under the royal tyranny that is bound to come? I leave you in slavery, and this thought alone will torment me at the last. I ought, instead, to advise you how patiently to bear your chains. But I cannot!

¹· Babeuf was arrested on 21 floréal (May 10, 1796). In the wave of hysteria that followed, hundreds of republicans were proscribed and arrested.

²· "Représentation nationale judiciaire." The Constitution of the year III (August, 1795) made provision for a High Court to try cases involving primarily high officials of the state. The jury before which such cases would be tried was to be elected annually by departmental or local assemblies throughout France. The judges and public prosecutors, seven in number, were selected by the Court of Cassation (Court of Appeals). Writs of indictment were not drawn by the prosecutors, but by the Council of Five Hundred (the lower house of the bicameral legislative body).

³· February 24, 1797.

⁴· October 5, 1795 was the day of the last great uprising of the Paris people, under royalist and Jacobin leadership, in protest against the reactionary Constitution of the year III proclaimed as the law of the land on September 23, 1795. The bloody suppression of this uprising by the Convention's general, Napoleon Bonaparte, paved the way for the dictatorial rule of the Directory.

⁵· Louis-Antoine de Saint-Just; see Biographical Notes.

⁶· Abbé Morelly; see Biographical Notes.

⁷· In 1750 the Academy of Dijon announced an essay competition on the theme: "Has the restoration of the arts and sciences had a purifying effect upon morals?" Rousseau's contribution, *Discourse on the Arts and Sciences,* won the prize and established his reputation in Parisian society as a writer.

⁸· Literally, Manifesto of Equals.

⁹· In 1753 Rousseau entered the Academy of Dijon's competition a second time with his essay, *Discourse on the Origin and Foundation of Inequality among Men.* This famous work was a direct attack on the cruel and unjust property arrangements of eighteenth-century society. It did not win the Academy's prize, as Babeuf states, but was published by its author in 1755.

¹⁰· The quotations which, in the following pages, Babeuf ascribes to Diderot were taken from the *Code de la Nature,* which was published in Amsterdam in 1773 under Diderot's name. Many years later it was proven that the real author of this very influential work was not Diderot, and that most likely it was composed by the Abbé Morelly.

¹¹· "Cette instabilité, ces vicissitudes périodiques des empires seraient-elles possibles là où tous les biens seraient indivisiblement communs?"

¹²· "Ne vaut-il pas mieux emporter la gloire de n'avoir pas survécu à la servitude?"

MANIFESTE DES EGAUX

BY SYLVAIN MARECHAL

PEOPLE OF FRANCE!

For fifteen hundred years you have lived in slavery and in misery. And for the last six years you have existed in the hourly expectation of independence, happiness, and equality.

Equality is the first principle of nature, the most elementary need of man, the prime bond of any decent association among human beings. But in this you, the French people, have fared no better than the rest of mankind. Humanity, the world over, has always been in the grip of more or less clever cannibals—creatures who have battened on men in order to advance their own selfish ambitions and to nourish their own selfish lust for power. Throughout man's history he has been gulled with fine words, he has received only the shadow of a promise, not its substance. Hypocrites, from time immemorial, have told us that *men are equal;* and yet monstrous and degrading inequality has, from time immemorial, ground humanity into the dust. Since the dawn of human history man has understood that equality is the finest ornament of the human condition, yet not once has he been successful in his struggles to bring his vision to life. Equality has remained a legal fiction, beautiful but baseless. And today, when we demand it with a new insistence, our rulers reply: "Silence! Real equality is an idle dream. Be content with equality before the law. Ignorant and lowborn herd, what else do you need?"

Men of high degree—lawmakers, rulers, the rich—now it is your turn to listen to us.

Men are equal. This is a self-evident truth. As soon say that it is night when the sun shines, as deny this.

Henceforth we shall live and die as we have been born—equal. Equality or death: that is what we want. And that is what we shall have, no matter what the price to be paid. Woe to you who stand in our way or try to thwart the realization of our dearest wish!

The French Revolution is only the forerunner of another, even greater, that shall finally put an end to the era of revolutions. The people have swept away the kings and priests who have been leagued against them.

Next they will sweep away the modern upstarts, the tyrants and tricksters who have usurped the ancient seats of power.

What else do we need other than equality before the law?

We need not only this equality as it is written down in the Declaration of the Rights of Man and of the Citizen; we need it in life, in our very midst, in our homes. For the true and living equality we will give up everything. Let the arts perish, if need be! But let us have real equality.

Men of high degree—lawmakers, rulers, the rich—strangers as you are to the love of man, to good faith, to compassion: it is no good to say that we are only "bringing up again the old cry of *loi agraire.*" It is our turn to speak. Listen to our just demands and to the law of nature which sanctions them.

The *loi agraire*—the division of the land—has been the instinctive demand of a handful of soldiers of fortune, of peoples here and there governed by passion, not by reason. We intend something far better and far more just: the COMMON GOOD, or the COMMUNITY OF GOODS. There must be an end to individual ownership of the land, for *the land is nobody's personal property*. Our demand is for the communal ownership of the earth's resources. *These resources are the property of mankind.*

We say that an end must be put to the situation in which the overwhelming majority of mankind, living under the thumb of a tiny minority, sweats and toils for the sole benefit of a few. In France fewer than a million persons own and dispose of wealth that rightfully belongs to twenty millions of their fellow men, to their fellow citizens.

There must be an end to this outrage! Will people in times to come even be able to conceive that such a situation ever existed? There must be an end to this unnatural division of society into rich and poor, into strong and weak, into masters and servants, into *rulers and ruled.*

Age and sex are the sole natural distinctions existing between men. All men have the same needs, all are endowed with the same faculties, all are warmed by the same sun, and all breathe the same air. Why then should not all receive an equal share of food and clothing—equal both in that

SYLVAIN MARECHAL

quantity and quality to which all shall be entitled?

But a howl arises from the sworn enemies of a truly natural order of things. "Anarchists! Demagogues!" they shriek. "You are nothing more than instigators of mob violence. That's what you are."

PEOPLE OF FRANCE,

We shall not waste time dignifying such charges with an answer. But to you we say: the high enterprise which we are engaged upon has a single purpose—to put an end to civil strife and to the sufferings of the masses.

No vaster plan than ours has ever been conceived or put into execution. Once in a long while men of vision have discussed it, cautiously and in whispers; none of them has had the boldness to speak out and to tell the whole truth.

The hour for decisive action has now struck. The people's suffering has reached its peak; it darkens the face of the earth. For centuries chaos has reigned under the name of "order." Now the time has come to mend matters. We, who love justice and who seek happiness—let us enter the struggle for the sake of equality. The time has come to establish THE REPUBLIC OF EQUALITY, to prepare an asylum for mankind. The time has come to set the earth to rights. You, who are oppressed, join us: come and partake of the feast which nature has provided for all her sons and daughters.

PEOPLE OF FRANCE,

A glorious and historic destiny has been reserved for you.

Hidebound tradition and blind prejudice will set barriers, as they always have, in the way of the establishment of the Republic of Equality. True equality—that alone provides for all human needs without sacrificing some men to the selfish interests of others—will not be welcome to everyone. Selfish and ambitious people will curse us. Men who have grown rich by thieving from their fellows will be the first to cry "thief." Proud men, living in privilege or in idleness, who have grown callous to the sufferings of others, will do battle with us. Men who wield arbitrary power, or who are its creatures, will not unprotesting bow their stiff necks beneath the yoke. The shape of things to come, the common good, their blind eyes cannot see. But how can a handful of such people prevail against a whole nation that has at last found the rapturous happiness it sought so long?

The day after the revolution for true equality has taken place people will be amazed. They will say: "The common good was so easy to attain! We only had to will it! Why on earth didn't we realize that sooner—why did we have to be told so often? It's absolutely true: when one man is richer and more powerful than the rest of us, everything is spoiled; crime and misery flourish."

PEOPLE OF FRANCE,

What is the hallmark of excellence in a constitution? Only true equality can serve as a foundation on which to base your Republic and satisfy all your needs. The aristocratic charters of 1791 and 1795 did not break your chains: they riveted them upon you more firmly. The Constitution of 1793 was a giant step toward true equality, the greatest that we have yet taken. It was dedicated to the goal of the common good, but did not, even so, fully provide the basis for organizing it.

PEOPLE OF FRANCE,

Open your eyes and hearts to full happiness: recognize the REPUBLIC OF EQUALITY. Join with us in working for it.

Babeuf's Defense before the High Court at Vendôme tries to achieve the impossible: recognition, by the established authority, of extreme civil disobedience as a legitimate protest against established authority. Insoluble contradiction: the representatives and protectors of law and order are supposed to give official, governmental approval to attempted subversion either by acquitting the defendants or by punishing them lightly. The facts were incontestable: Babeuf had engaged in subversion by word and deed; he had openly advocated the overthrow of the established system; he had conspired to organize armed insurrection. His actions could hardly be justified by his argument that the Constitution of 1795 which was to be the legal, democratic basis of the government had been adopted only by about 900,000 votes[1] and under "dubious circumstances," whereas the Montagnard Constitution of 1793 had received about 4,800,000 votes "cast freely."[2] For within the parliamentary framework, even rigged elections, if not successfully contested, are elections—expressions of popular sovereignty and thus constitutional. Babeuf knew all this, and he drew the conclusion: he had to admit the fact of the conspiracy while insisting that it was not a real conspiracy. And he did so by appealing from the rules of representative (parliamentary) democracy to the power of direct (popular) democracy, from the (apparent) sovereignty of the people to the true interest of the people.

This strategy, which, in one form or another, has become an essential part of all theories of revolutionary dictatorship, is, in Babeuf's Defense, based on the notion that the people who vote for their constitution and their representatives are not necessarily the sovereign people, that their expressed will is not necessarily their autonomous will, that their free choice is not necessarily freedom. In Babeuf's words: the people might be misled; they might, "with apparent freedom, have adopted a radically vicious Constitution" (p. 14).[3] And: "lack of proper information might have prevented them from recognizing this" (ibid.). In this case, the people would have acted against their "own true interests"—against themselves. The weakness and ignorance of the people would cause them to be subject to the powers that be and popular sovereignty would thus be susceptible to administration. Under such circumstances, even a free vote could be a vote for servitude, and democracy could become a system of domination and exploitation by consent. To Babeuf, consent obtained in this manner is annulled, is no consent, and government by

EDME-LOUIS-BARTHELEMY BAILLY

the people must be achieved in the struggle against the people who consented to servitude. Moreover, the establishment of democracy would mean subversion of the established democracy—just as it meant subversion of the established Ancien Regime.

Here, of course, the question immediately arises: according to what criteria or standards can the expression of the popular will be determined as misled, deceived, false?

The problem is already distorted and obscured if it is formulated in personal terms; if one asks: who determines the distinction between true and false interests? For the problem is not one of persons (or groups of persons) but of objective and demonstrable criteria; once they are defined, the respective historical situation will determine which social groups could adopt these criteria and act accordingly. The argument that such criteria, if they exist at all, are already invalidated because they would be those of an "elite," a minority, begs the question since it assumes that the majority is *eo ipso* right. In any case, for Babeuf and his friends, the true interests of the people had been defined on two levels: in theory by the philosophy of the Enlightenment which had prepared the intellectual ground for the democratization of society; and in practice by the situation of the poor people after the Thermidor. In theory, the criteria for the harmony of an established social order with the true interests of the people were the realization of the inalienable rights of man as stated in the "ageless book of nature." And the most basic of these rights is every man's striving to improve his lot, to satisfy his needs, to have an equal share in the social wealth. Human society was founded for this goal; the welfare of all its members is the sole reason for the social contract. If a state of affairs has come into existence where the masses are forced "into a life of toil and hunger, and obliged, in blood and tears, to maintain a handful of privileged beings in idleness and profligacy," then the social contract is abrogated, and the people can demand its restoration (p. 26). Legitimacy then lies only in the attempt to restore the broken contract against those who broke it: where there is no society, there can be no subversion of society. Babeuf's insurrection was supposed to bring about order, not disorder, and if his conspiracy aimed at the restoration of order, it was not a crime but "the height of virtue" (p. 13).

In the light of this theory, Babeuf re-examines the concepts of popular sovereignty and of conspiracy, delving beneath their ideological obfuscation. This is the central part of his Defense, and its historical significance far transcends the specific circumstances under which his trial took place. He distinguishes three definitions of conspiracy: (1) intent to overthrow established governments, (2) intent to overthrow a Constitution freely adopted by the people, (3) intent to overthrow legitimate authority. The first is quickly shown to be erroneous: it would mean that the people would always have to remain under the prevailing form of government, "no matter how base and vile" it would be—a flagrant violation of the principle of popular sovereignty and of the inalienable rights of man. Babeuf has also already refuted the second definition of conspiracy by his argument that in oppressive conditions the people might freely adopt a Constitution which is against their own interests. There remains the third definition, the only one which Babeuf accepts: only a government which recognizes man's inalienable rights and governs in accordance with the principles of popular sovereignty can claim to be legitimate authority. A conspiracy against such a government "would indeed constitute a truly subversive act" (p. 15). And Babeuf now can easily argue that the government against which he conspired is no such legitimate authority. For the Constitution of 1795 did away with universal suffrage and popular sovereignty in legislation, restored the distinction between active and passive citizens, abolished civil rights sanctioned by the democratic Constitution of 1793, and vested the executive with powers removed from popular control (p. 17). Under these circumstances, legitimacy was not with the defenders of this government, but with the conspirators against it.

This reasoning and the conception of inalienable rights based on natural law have been challenged many times, mainly on the grounds that the existence of such natural law is not demonstrable, that it is therefore ambiguous and subject to arbitrary definitions, so that it can serve as a justification for any power, reactionary as well as revolutionary. But this argument does not seem to have bothered Babeuf. There is a point where demonstration other than "seeing" becomes impossible, not because the things to be seen are too distant, too obscure, too nebulous, doubtful, but on the contrary: because they are wholly clear, direct, close—indeed self-evident. The right to satisfy vital needs, to improve one's lot are in this sense self-evident—the rest is academic semantics. The real difficulty, the doubts begin when the realm of the necessities of life, the satisfaction of vital needs is transcended. Can one legislate, legitimately and in the name of the common welfare, in the realm of "luxuries" and of intellectual culture? For Babeuf, this question did not arise: it was simply a matter of the necessities, their equal distribution, and the establishment of a government willing and capable of undertaking such distribution, that is, for Babeuf, building a communist society.

Communism looms large in Babeuf's Defense; he presents it as the only "natural" society organized for the common good. He cites as witnesses spokesmen of the revolutionary government of 1793-1794; he cites Morelly (attributing the *Code de la Nature* to Diderot), Mably, Rousseau. Babeuf's communism is a primitive, even repressive form of egalitarianism—there is no need to discuss its merits or its chances of finding popular support. In the manifesto of the Equals calling for the insurrection there is no mention of communism. Mathiez has drawn attention to this fact,[4] and to the even more surprising one that the subscribers to Babeuf's revolutionary journal (which did advocate communism) came in large part from the class of bankers, financiers, manufacturers, high officials, functionaries, professionals.[5] Associated in various degrees with the Jacobin dictatorship, these sympathizers supported the leftist opposition against the Directoire because of the threat of new waves of White Terror against the Jacobins. One wonders what would have become of Babeuf's communism if his conspiracy had had at least initial success: would these forces on the Right (who had followed the Tribune of the People not because but in spite of his communism) have taken over and perhaps accelerated the development of bourgeois society in France, "skipping" the costly Napoleonic stage?

Babeuf indeed had no effective support from the Left. In his Defense, he recurrently speaks of the lack of mass support (p. 11); the "paralysis of popular initiative" (p. 19); and he sums up: "As a matter of fact, I was very far from enjoying any measure of popular support" (p. 27). The catastrophic deterioration of the economy, the growing inequality, and the conspicuous corruption had turned popular sentiment against the Republic. The royalist reaction had gained momentum, and it was in fact under royalist leadership that the last great popular uprising had occurred (13 vendémiaire 1795). The people seemed "resigned and ready to go once more under the despot's yoke," they were "weary of a Revolution whose twists and turns had brought them only sorrow," they had "turned back to royalism" (pp. 19, 20). Familiar historical situation: the tribune of the people must teach the people that the Republic which they have and detest is "not the real Republic," that the "Revolution is not over," and that, if it is "brought to an end in mid-passage, it will be judged by

100

HONORE DE MIRABEAU

history as little more than a catalogue of bloody crimes" (p. 21). Thus the "bloody crimes" must be redeemed by continuing the revolution to the end. For Babeuf, the beginning of the end is the enactment of the democratic Constitution of 1793; the end is the communist society; the means, under the given circumstances: the armed insurrection. And because the people for whom the revolution is to be made are deceived, hostile, or apathetic, it will be a revolution by a minority, that means, it will involve the Terror—against the enemies of the revolution, who would presumably include the deceived and misled people in whose interest the revolution is to be carried through. Here is Article 12 of the *Acte d'insurrection:*

Toute opposition sera vaincue sur-le-champs par la force. Les opposants seront exterminés.

Seront également mis à mort:

Ceux qui battront ou feront battre la générale;

Les étrangers de quelque nation qu'ils soient, qui seront trouvés dans les rues; Tous les présidents, secrétaires et commandants de la conspiration royale de vendémiaire qui oseraient aussi se mettre en évidence.[6]

But Babeuf makes a distinction between legitimate and illegitimate Terror. The former is characterized by the fact that it is not indiscriminate, that it respects the rights granted to the defendants by a revolutionary legislation, and that it is exercised only to protect the revolution and the welfare of the people. This distinction may explain Babeuf's apparently contradictory attitude towards Terror. In his pre-conspiratorial days, he had joined the Thermidorians in denouncing Robespierre to whom he attributed a sinister system of depopulation of France in order to meet the threat of mass starvation. He had also attacked, in the most uncompromising terms, the horrible terroristic activities of Carrier at Nantes. And yet, in the same pamphlet, he wrote that he would not hesitate "to strike with capital punishment" all enemies of the people *soit qu'ils le ruinent dans sa fortune, qu'ils l'affament par de sordides spéculations, qu'ils l'assassinent par la trahison ou par le fer, et surtout s'ils méconnaissent sa souveraineté, s'ils attentent à sa liberté.*[7]

And he approved of the acquittal of the terrorist co-defendants of Carrier, saying:

je n'ai vu en eux, excepté le régulateur suprême de leurs actes et de leurs volontés, que des amans passionés de la liberté, déplorant leurs fureurs.[8]

Legitimate Terror must be practiced without revenge and cruelty, solely in protection of the people against their enemies. Again, the elusive notion "welfare of the people" seems to be the sole criterion for the legitimacy of Terror. However, we can now define this notion more clearly. For Babeuf, "the people" are not the people at large, the "population" of the Republic, not even all its citizens, but only the poor, the downtrodden, the hungry. And their welfare can be defined clearly: it is the alleviation of their poverty, the abolition of their exploitation, the satisfaction of their hunger. And under the conditions prevailing at the time, this goal could only be attained by suppressing the powers and institutions which opposed a radical redistribution of power and wealth. "The man who wills an end also wills the means to gain that end" (p. 25). Moreover, this legitimate Terror is democracy in action because the poor people on whose behalf it is exercised are the majority of the people. If they do not spontaneously *act* as majority because they are "misled" or kept in ignorance or deprived of the means to act effectively, the revolution —their revolution—must needs become the concern of the leadership: it must become a dictatorship for though not by the majority.

Did Babeuf ever believe that he could convince his judges of the strength of his argument that legitimacy was on the side of his conspiracy rather than of the authorities who prosecuted him? The tenor of his speech, and particularly his concluding remarks, suggest a negative answer. His last words, and the horrible scenes following the pronouncement of the death sentence are the most telling indictment of a revolution betrayed and a people forced into apathy and compliance. In the light of this hell of helplessness and futility, Babeuf's long invocation of the radical ideology of the time assumes heightened significance. The ideas of Reason and Freedom, the analysis of the origin of inequality and exploitation, the insistence on the inalienable rights of man —these were ideas praised throughout the country and beyond its frontiers, enshrined in the great mausoleum of culture and progress. But at the same time, the attempt to connect the words with deeds, to define the meaning of these ideas in terms of action which would translate ideology into reality was, in various degrees, subjected to discrimination, persecution, suppression. Thus only the ideology remained intact: it could be transmitted to future generations and serve as guide in the preparation for future struggles.

The message of Babeuf's strategy was not lost. The theoretical underpinning of his conspiracy was the identification of "the people" with the poor people, and the identification of the poor people with the majority of the people—

the majority which, precisely because of the condition in which it was kept, was not capable of acting by itself and for itself—as majority. In various forms, this conception has been operative in all continental revolutionary movements from the Jacobins to the Bolsheviks. But with the increasing democratization of industrial society, it becomes increasingly difficult to maintain this identification. The number of the "poor" in Babeuf's sense tends to decline until it becomes, in the most advanced societies, a minority of the population. And "the people" comes to mean "all the people," equal "before the law" regardless of social status and occupation. Then, the "welfare" or "interest" of the people can no longer be defined without internal contradictions, because the interest of one class is not that of another, and each class has an equal right to be counted. Moreover, the concept of a general welfare and "true" interest ceases to be a goal to be attained only through revolutionary changes; the common welfare and the true interest of the people are supposed to assert themselves in the normal functioning of the democratic process.

But while this development may make the traditional concept of revolution obsolete, it only throws into sharper relief Babeuf's argument that any invocation of democracy, the will of the people, popular sovereignty, becomes questionable, nay invalid, if the people, the majority of the people are "misled," or indoctrinated, or not acquainted with the essential facts. Where such conditions prevail, the democracy is still spurious—in Babeuf's words: the Republic is not yet the "real Republic," and its establishment would involve acting (and writing) against the people, against the majority. For the democratization of society, even where it has reached the stage of universal suffrage and equality before the law, and free choices in the sphere of consumption, does not preclude domination, indoctrination, and manipulation—and the less so where the technological and economic concentration of power leads to a factual monopoly or oligopoly in the means of mass communication. Then the condition which Babeuf faced: the "falsification" of popular sovereignty in the name of popular sovereignty would still prevail—but obfuscated and enlarged beyond the reaches of any conspiracy "from the Left." And a theory and strategy which was quite unrealistic but not utopian in 1796 appears as utterly utopian today.

[1]The figure given by Albert Mathiez, *La Réaction Thermidorienne* (Paris, Colin, 1929), p. 300, is 1,057,390 votes.

[2]Mathiez' figure: 1,801,918.

[3]Page numbers in parenthesis refer to the text of the Defense.

[4]*Le Directoire* (Paris, Colin, 1934), p. 207.

[5]*Ibid.*, pp. 192 f.

[6]"All opposition will be crushed at once by force; hostile elements will be executed. Those who sound the call to arms, or cause it to be sounded, will also be put to death; likewise foreigners, regardless of nationality, who are found in the streets, and any of the leadership of the royal conspiracy of Vendémiaire who show themselves in public." Buonarotti, *Conspiration pour l'égalité dite de Babeuf* (Paris, Editions Sociales, 1957), II, 168.

[7]"...who pillage its wealth, drive it into destitution by speculative operations, destroy it by treason or the sword; and, above all, who spit upon its sovereignty and seek to undermine its freedom." Babeuf, *Du Système de dépopulation...*(Paris, 1795), p. 187.

[8]"I deplored their fury; but, leaving aside the central determinant of their behavior, I saw in them only men passionately dedicated to the cause of freedom." *Ibid.*, pp. 193 f.

AGIS. Spartan prince and reformer, who tried to effect an end to wealth, luxury, and inequality by means of redivision of the land and a return to a simple communal life. He was executed by his political enemies, led by Leonidas, in 240 B.C.

ANYTUS. Athenian orator and popular leader, was the principal accuser of Socrates, and, with Meletus (q.v.), the architect of Socrates' trial and condemnation. His name has become a symbol for basely motivated attack upon genius.

ARMAND. See Harmand.

BORDES, Charles (1711–81). Born in Lyon, was a *philosophe*, playwright, and member of the Academy of Lyon. He wrote the *Discours sur les avantages des sciences et des arts* (1750), a refutation of Rousseau's prize essay of 1750, *Discours sur les sciences et les arts,* and was the author of numerous other works.

BAILLY, Edmé-Louis-Barthélemy (1760–1819). Public prosecutor at the trial of Babeuf and his associates, was a member of the Council of 500 and one of the fiercest opponents of Jacobinism. Later he became a supporter of Bonaparte and was made a Baron of the Empire.

BARNEVELDT, Jan Van Olden (1547–1619). Dutch statesman who became grand pensionary of Holland in 1586 and negotiated the treaty with Spain in 1609 following the War of Independence. Siding with the Remonstrants against the Calvinists, he was arrested by Maurice of Nassau in 1618 and condemned to death for treason by a packed court.

BUONARROTI, Filippo Michele (1761–1837). Of aristocratic origins, born in Pisa, where he studied law, absorbed the advanced ideas of the Enlightenment, and took fire from the reforming spirit then abroad in Tuscany. At the outbreak of the French Revolution, Buonarroti exiled himself in the French province of Corsica and engaged there in fervid political agitation. In 1793 he visited Paris, became affiliated with the Jacobins, and received the post of commissioner for Oneglia (Maritime Alps), occupied by French troops in 1794. In 1795 the Directory recalled him to Paris, and in March of that year placed him in the *Prison du Plessis;* there he established relationships that led him, on his release in October 1795, to join the Babouvists and to become one of the leaders of the *Conjuration.* Arrested and tried with Babeuf and the other conspirators, he was sentenced to deportation and imprisonment. Many years later, living in Paris in his impoverished old age, Buonarroti wrote and published the *Conspiration pour l'égalité dite de Babeuf* (Brussels, 1828), which retains much value as an account of the organizational structure and revolutionary activities of the *Conjura-*

tion. Some modern Italian students have claimed Buonarroti as the leading theorist of the Babouvist movement. This is debatable.

CATO, Marcus Porcius (95–46 B.C.). A Stoic and republican, he opposed political corruption and fought for the preservation of the Republic against Caesar. When Caesar triumphed he stabbed himself rather than live under a tyranny.

DARTHE, Augustin Aléxandre. Jacobin leader from the Pas de Calais and member of the secret directorate of the *Conjuration. des Égaux.* Refusing during the Vendôme trial to admit the authority of the court or to speak in his own defense, he was condemned to death and executed with Babeuf.

DIDEROT, Denis (1713–84). Editor of the *Encyclopedia,* philosopher, man of letters, and one of the boldest speculative minds of the eighteenth century. The *Code de la Nature,* from which Babeuf quotes extensively, was for many years attributed to Diderot, though its real author was probably Abbé Morelly (q.v.).

DROUET, Jean-Baptiste (1763–1824). The postmaster of Sainte-Menehould who recognized Louis XVI in his flight from France in 1791, and had him arrested at Varennes. Elected to the Convention in 1792, he voted for the King's death. He fought in the revolutionary armies, was taken prisoner and, returning to France in 1795, became one of the leaders of the Babouvist movement. He escaped trial by flight and lived to become prefect of Sainte-Menehould under the Empire.

GERMAIN, Charles. Born at Narbonne in 1770, was a student in Paris at the outbreak of the Revolution, took service as a soldier, became an officer in the service of the Republic, and was broken, demoted, and arrested by the thermidoreans for his Jacobin views. He was imprisoned in 1795 at Arras, and established there his association with Babeuf. Liberated at the end of August that same year, Germain threw himself into activity for the restoration of the Constitution of 1793; when the *conjuration* came into being he was charged with revolutionary work in the army. He was tried at Vendôme and condemned to deportation.

GRACCHUS, Tiberius and Caius. The Gracchi were members of the Roman nobility who placed themselves at the head of the peasant movement for land distribution. Tiberius was elected the people's tribune in 134 B.C., and proceeded to submit legislation providing, among other things, for the creation of unalienable homesteads out of the latifundia. He was assassinated by his political enemies in B.C. 132; Caius suffered a like fate eleven years later when he attempted to resume his brother's work.

HARMAND, Jean Baptiste. Was a member of the National Convention, 1792–5. On April 17, 1793, he spoke to the house on the Girondin plan for a republican Constitution. Babeuf quotes *verbatim* from this speech (*Archives parlementaires* LXII, 270 ff.).

HELVETIUS, Claude Adrien (1715–71). French philosopher, famous principally for *De l'esprit* (1758) and *De l'homme* (1770). Helvetius taught that innate intelligence in human beings is the same for all. Observed differences are purely the result of differences in education. This assumption underlies the emphasis that Babeuf placed upon education as a national resource to be available equally to all members of society.

KOSCIUSKO, Tadeusz (1746–1817). Polish patriot who served the American revolutionary cause, 1776–83. Returning to Poland, he fought for the democratic constitution of 1791, and, on the second partition of his country in 1793, withdrew to Leipzig. He became commander in chief of the Polish insurgents against the Tsar in 1794; defeated at the battle of Maciejowice, he was taken prisoner and sent for two years to St. Petersburg. Most of the rest of his life was passed in exile.

LE PELETIER DE SAINT-FARGEAU, Ferdinand-Louis-Félix (1767–1837). Wealthy Jacobin, half brother of the Revolution's first martyr, Michel Le Peletier (q.v.), was one of Babeuf's intimate friends and political associates. Of noble birth, he was raised by his parents with an army career in mind; but the coming of the Revolution thrust him into politics. Both he and his brother were representative of the idealistic young nobility who forsook family traditions and aligned themselves with the revolutionary cause. Admitted to the Jacobin club in 1793, Le Peletier suffered proscription when Robespierre was overthrown; and was one of the first to be attracted to the leadership of Babeuf and Buonarroti (q.v.) in the struggle that began in 1795 for the overthrow of the reactionary *Directoire* and for a return to the principles of the Jacobin Republic: a struggle that came to a climax with the work of the *Conjuration des Égaux*.

When Babeuf was arrested in May 1796, Le Peletier was hopelessly compromised in the mass of documentary evidence then seized. He was arrested and fled, possibly with the Government's connivance, was placed on trial at Vendôme *in absentia*, and acquitted. After Babeuf's execution, Le Peletier adopted his friend's son Émile and lived on in opposition, in exile and in prison, haunted in empty and difficult days by the passionate memories of revolutionary action and the republican dream.

LE PELETIER DE SAINT-FAR-

GEAU, Louis-Michel (1760–93). Sat in the Estates General of 1789 as a representative of the nobility; as a member of the Constituent Assembly, he voted for the decree of June 19, 1790 that abolished the First Estate. As a member of the Convention, he voted for the death of Louis XVI on January 16, 1793 and was assassinated on January 20 by one of the ex-king's bodyguards. He thus became the French Republic's first martyr. Was a half-brother of Félix Le Peletier (q.v.).

LINDET, Jean-Baptiste-Robert (1746–1825). Lawyer, moderate Jacobin, and member both of the Legislative Assembly and of the Convention. He drew up the report which formed the basis for Louis XVI's indictment. As a member of the Committee for Public Safety under the Terror he was responsible for the distribution of food supplies.

LYCURGUS. Legendary lawgiver of early Sparta. He is credited with having introduced a communist regime and having made a division of the lands that did away with social inequality. The constitution which he gave to Sparta is alleged to have procured the Spartan state's military and political ascendancy. All of this is said to have occurred in the ninth century B.C.

MABLY, Gabriel Bonnot de (1709–85). Mably embarked on a diplomatic career in the service of the French Crown, but retired in early middle age to write a series of historical and philosophic works, a collected edition of which was published in Paris 1794–5. He attacked the institution of private property in all its forms and is regarded as one of the forerunners of the modern socialist movement.

MACHIAVELLI, Niccolo (1469–1527). Florentine statesman and Italian patriot, author of the celebrated political treatise, *The Prince* (1515).

MANLIUS, Marcus. Roman consul, hero of the defense of the Capitol against the Gauls in the invasion of 390 B.C. Championing the demands of the *plebs,* he fell victim to the hatred of the aristocracy. He was accused of plotting the violent overthrow of the Republic, tried, condemned, and hurled from the Tarpeian Rock.

MARECHAL, Sylvain (1750–1803). Revolutionary agitator, journalist, poet, and militant atheist, was a member of the secret directorate of the *conjuration,* and author of the celebrated *Manifeste des Égaux* setting forth Babouvist objectives. Maréchal was neither arrested nor indicted for his role in the conspiracy.

MARGAROT, Maurice. Was a London merchant and champion of parliamentary reform. Delegated in 1793 by the London Corresponding

Society to the British Convention in Edinburgh summoned to demand parliamentary reform, Margarot was indicted for sedition and sentenced in 1794 to transportation and fourteen years' confinement in a penal colony.

MELETUS. Athenian, one of the principal accusers of Socrates.

MEUSE, Armand de la. See Armand.

MORELLY, Abbé. Reputed author of the *Code de la Nature*, a celebrated utopian tract first published in Amsterdam in 1773 as part of a five-volume edition of works ascribed to Denis Diderot (q.v.). Almost nothing is known concerning Morelly's life.

ROUSSEAU, Jean-Jacques (1712–78). Political theorist, philosopher, educator, and essayist, among the greatest of the French eighteenth-century men of letters. He foreshadowed much that came to fruition in the French Revolution, whose theorist *par excellence* he was. Though driven into exile in 1762 as a result of the publication of *Émile*, much of Rousseau's most radical writing—*Contrat social, La nouvelle Héloïse, Discours sur l'origine de l'inégalité parmi les hommes*—was done in France, where he spent more than half his adult life.

SAINT-JUST, Louis-Antoine de (1767–94). Jacobin leader from the Nivernais, friend and political associate of Maximilien Robespierre, and member of the National Convention, was one of the guiding spirits of the Committee of Public Safety that ruled France 1793–4 and that thrust back France's enemies from her frontiers. When the thermidorian reaction set in he was guillotined along with Robespierre.

SOCRATES (469–399 B.C.). Athenian stonecutter and philosopher, was put on trial in his old age on a charge of denying the gods and corrupting the youth. Socrates' disciple, Plato, reported the defense that his master made in one of the most brilliant of his dialogues, *The Apology*. Of the existence of this dialogue Babeuf seems not to have been aware.

SYDNEY, Algernon (1622–82). Republican of noble birth, Sydney took up arms against Charles I in 1644 on behalf of "the rights of mankind, the laws of this land, and the true protestant religion." He was arrested in 1682 for his part in plotting insurrection against Charles II in the Rye House Plot, tried before Chief Justice Jeffreys, and executed.

TALLIEN, Jean-Lambert (1769–1820). Secretary-general of the Paris *commune* in 1792, and, for a while, an ardent Jacobin. Tallien changed course sharply in 1794 when he dissolved the revolutionary and military tribunals in Bordeaux and helped bring Robespierre to the scaffold. He was of humble origins, and his turn toward conservatism seems to have been hastened by the relations he entertained with a royalist lady, Marquise de Fontenay, known as Thérèsia Cabarrus.

WELDON, James. Was a soldier in His Majesty's Seventh Regiment of Irish Dragoons. In 1795 he was tried and convicted of high treason for revolutionary activity against the Crown. Execution took place in Dublin in January, 1796.

YOUNG, Arthur (1741–1820). English agriculturist, traveler, and writer, visited France for a total of six months during the period 1787–90. His classic *Travels in France* appeared in 1792–4, and painted a somber but vivid picture of rural life under the old regime.

GRACCHUS BABEUF

GRACCHUS BABEUF

ANACHARSIS CLOOTS